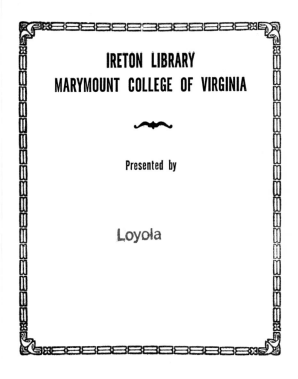

*An Integrated
Development Strategy*

An Integrated
Development Strategy

Gisèle Asplund and **Göran Asplund**

Stockholm School of Economics

1807 1982

JOHN WILEY & SONS
Chichester · New York · Brisbane · Toronto · Singapore

Copyright © 1982 by John Wiley & Sons Ltd.

Library of Congress Cataloging in Publication Data:

Asplund, Gisèle, 1940–
   An integrated development strategy.
   Includes index.
   1. Industrial management.   2. Corporate planning.
   3. Organizational change.
   I. Asplund, Göran, 1943–   . II. Title.

HD38.A736   658.4′06   81-14822

ISBN 0 471 10075 7   AACR2

British Library Cataloguing in Publication Data:

Asplund, Gisèle
   An integrated development strategy.
   1. Corporate planning
   I. Title II. Asplund, Göran
   658.4′01   HD30.28

ISBN 0 471 10075 7

Typeset by Pintail Studios Ltd, Ringwood, Hampshire
Printed at The Pitman Press, Bath.

To Chris Argyris

Contents

Preface

We started working on the ideas presented in this book ten years ago in a small whitewashed house on the island of Patmos in Greece. We had come to the island for recreation and work; one night as we sat discussing and analysing a recent assignment, we had our own small revelation – sitting, as it happened, in a vineyard about a hundred yards from the spot where the Revelation of St. John the Divine is said to have been written. Our revelation can be stated very simply: to understand fully what happens when a group of people formulate a business strategy, it is necessary to examine both rational decision-making processes and group dynamics, and to integrate insights from both these areas. But it still took almost ten years of hard work before we had made the necessary synthesis of diverse theoretical fragments and the vital intervention processes that ultimately brought us to what we have called an integrated development strategy, or IDS.

Of course we were not occupied solely with IDS during these ten years; two children joined us, Louise now eight years old and Daniel four. They have helped and encouraged us in our efforts to understand the nature of learning, never ceasing to supply us with fascinating problems to solve.

Another person who has inspired and helped us all along is Professor Chris Argyris of Harvard University, USA. In his writings we have found a never-ending source of inspiration and wisdom, as well as a continual intellectual challenge. Thanks to a generous grant from the Wallenberg Foundation and the Stockholm School of Economics we were also able to stay with him at Harvard from 1974 to 1976. By this time we knew where we were heading, but without Chris Argyris' personal reactions, suggestions and guidance we would have been lost, because although our integrated development strategy solved some old problems it also seemed to create as many new ones. But there was a way out of the tunnel and Chris Argyris could always throw some light on the path so that we could find our way.

We have also benefited greatly from interesting discussions with our colleagues at the Stockholm School of Economics. Professor Folke Kristensson and Professor Gunnar Westerlund not only acted as our research advisors; they also took the trouble to read some of our working papers at a stage when considerable patience and good eyesight were needed to be able to make them out at all.

Professor Erik Johnsen of the Copenhagen School of Economics and Business Administration has also provided us with valuable comments and suggestions.

Nancy Adler has helped us to make the text more readable to an English-speaking public and we are most grateful for her competent work and moral support in producing the final version of the book.

Birgitta Beijbom and Myra Frigieri have typed the various versions with patience and efficiency.

Needless to say the clients with whom we have worked over the last few years have been of the greatest importance to our study. We have had the good fortune to work with some very intelligent and courageous managers who were not afraid to engage themselves in new directions – something which always calls for a good measure of trust. We owe them a debt for the confidence which they showed in us.

The integrated development strategy as described in this book brings together the academic disciplines of business policy and organizational learning and presupposes an intervention approach. Much work remains to be done, however, before a more general intervention theory can be developed to include even other academic disciplines such as operations research, managerial systems, etc.

We firmly believe that, although the road seems a long one, a general theory of intervention is attainable; and the route to be followed is a fascinating one. Not only is there much to learn along the way since every step is by its very nature a unique learning experience; but in addition to this you never know exactly what direction you will be going in next.

We hope that in the following pages our readers will find encouragement to take the risks necessary for planning and promoting their own future learning.

We dedicate the book to Chris Argyris.

PART I

Theory

CHAPTER 1

Towards an Integrated Development Strategy

Background to the Integrated Development Strategy (IDS)

The need for IDS

Why do some corporations grow and become prosperous while others fail and die? This is one of the questions at the core of all management theory. A question that follows from this is: How do the successful companies manage their operations and what specific qualities help to make them successful? And the opposite question: What do unsuccessful companies do wrong?

One of the most common answers to these questions is that successful companies find ways of adapting to changing market conditions and changing technologies, while unsuccessful companies do not. But this answer is unfortunately of little or no guidance to people preoccupied with the creation of corporate or business strategies or with the development of technological or organizational systems. Such people are not helped by abstract recommendations on the lines of 'Seek market opportunities that match your special organizational strengths'. They can understand the wisdom of this for themselves. Instead they need concrete guidance in tackling a variety of problems. They may ask: 'How should we design a strategy formulation process?' 'How can we create an environment in which people work together instead of trying to do one another down?' 'What models and concepts can help us to choose our main strategic actions at a particular time?' 'How can we create an organizational climate favourable to change and learning?'

In this book we shall try to answer these and other questions and in so doing we shall introduce a method which we have called the integrated development strategy or IDS.

The idea underlying IDS is that all development work in organizations must focus simultaneously on technical questions such as corporate strategy, marketing, organizational structure, administrative systems, *and* on behavioural questions such as organizational culture, norms, behavioural modes, communication styles etc. Further, we argue that the integration of these two approaches does not occur spontaneously; it requires a special way of thinking and a special way of working.

3

IDS involves not only a theory for the integration of task and behaviour. It also comprises a way of looking at both the technical and the behavioural fields that is partly new. And new concepts are needed if we want to create a holistic approach instead of a series of partial theories based on knowledge from specialist academic disciplines.

Some personal experiences that led to the development of IDS

In 1970 one of the authors of this book was engaged to act as marketing consultant to a firm. A session was arranged at which some of the top line executives were to discuss market segmentation and marketing mix together with the consultant and the marketing director. By the end of the first day the consultant had told the group all there was to know about market segmentation; he had presented cases of successful and unsuccessful segmentation and encouraged the executives to discuss their own strategies on a basis of a manual reproduced in a well-known textbook in this field.

The executives proved unusually knowledgeable about marketing theory. They produced an intelligent analysis of the case material, and the discussion based on the manual was also of a high intellectual standard.

Up to a point the consultant felt pleased, but he also had a nagging feeling that something was not quite right. Why had they hired a marketing expert, when their own ideas were already so advanced? The consultant's suspicions were further aroused after dinner, which they had all enjoyed together. One of the line executives approached him and said: 'Don't take this personally – but all we did today was actually quite useless. We've done it many times before and we will do it again. And we are all of us sufficiently smart to hold an intelligent discussion in the abstract, without ever touching on our real problems. We all recognize the dangerous areas. We discuss them frequently in smaller groups and we form secret alliances and so on. But none of these questions will come out into the open by talking about market segmentation.' When they all met again the next morning, the consultant brought up the question of communications in the group. But this discussion came to nothing; they all claimed that relations were excellent and there was no trouble about collaborating in a constructive way. And so the intelligent but superficial analysis continued, and the marketing seminar had very little impact on future marketing action.

At the same time the other author of this book was having a similar experience as a management consultant working on the development of a budget system.

In this case the company had created a group with members from different departments. According to management the cross-company composition of the group had several purposes: to help to achieve the best solution technically speaking, and to ensure that the solution had firm roots in the organization.

The group's aim was to develop a computer-controlled budget system for the company, and it had the following members:

- two members of the computer department (experts as regards technical solutions)
- two members of the production departments (users of the control system)
- a staff representative from the production departments (representing lower-level staff)
- a representative of the finance department (expert on the design of the control system)
- a consultant (who was to supply theoretical expertise and the unprejudiced eyes of an outsider).

Almost straightaway two camps formed. The computer representatives and the representative of the finance department formed a united front, recommending a particular way of attacking the problem, while the production department members and the employee representative formed another faction which, because it was unable to formulate a joint alternative to the suggestion of the others, devoted itself mainly to slowing down and delaying the whole job.

Mistrust and defensive attitudes were so strong that no-one dared bring up the problem of the sluggish collaboration in the group itself. But news of its inefficiency and meagre results gradually began to leak out, reaching management at a quarterly meeting with the trade union representatives. In a discussion on commission and the possibility of new principles for wage-setting – issues that were dependent on the recommended budget system – the trade union members asked about the progress of the budget project. Management then realized that the budget group had not produced any fruitful solutions, although it had been at work for more than six months. In fact no progress had been made at all, although the internal experts and the consultant had both made various suggestions, some innovative and some more conventional, about how to solve the company's problem.

Experiences like these made us ask ourselves whether there might not be ways of tackling the behavioural aspects, which would help to make the technical problem solving more effective. In the cases quoted we, as consultants, had obviously not succeeded in getting beneath the surface and grasping the really difficult problems, although we had put on a good show as seminar leaders and experts. While we were experiencing difficulties in trying to make technical problem solving more effective, we became aware of various approaches to organizational development (OD). As teachers we began to use the works of McGregor, Argyris, Bennis, Schein, and others. We had our own experience of laboratory research, and we also helped on various occasions to arrange OD programmes in organizations. Eventually we grew increasingly enthusiastic about the potential of OD. However, we also felt that the laboratory approach to learning about organizations was inadequate as a means of producing real change in organizational life. In organizations people act through the medium of budgets, market plans, programmes for technical development, etc. and the kind of behaviour that this involves in real organizational life was simply not being captured by ordinary OD programmes.

We also felt that people treated their OD experiences with great respect, but that they were seldom able to change their behaviour in their everyday setting. Life at the office continued more or less as before.

In light of these experiences we began trying to use our knowledge of behavioural science, and the models and techniques belonging to it, while working on purely technical matters such as corporate planning, marketing strategy, administrative systems and the like. We also tried to integrate the relevant task issues, when we were engaged to collaborate in behavioural organizational development projects.

Before turning to our model of development – IDS – we should first mention some of the writers who have given us intellectual guidance and inspiration.

Antecedents of the Integrated Development Strategy

Two broad lines of research and practice have been followed in attempts to find ways of improving organizational adaptiveness to a changing environment. One focuses on *organizational strategy formulation:* how do organizations evolve processes to facilitate their adaptation to a changing environment? The other focuses on *organizational learning and development:* how do organizations evolve processes to encourage learning and development in the face of a changing environment? Common to these two traditions is the problem they want to solve. But their frames of reference, and the models and methods which they use, are very different. Let us look a little more closely at what the two approaches really involve.

Strategy formulation

One way of coping with environmental change has been to design formal strategic planning systems.

Ansoff (1965), as the subtitle of his book suggests, followed 'an analytical approach to business policy for growth and expansion'. He was concerned to provide executives with tools for the formulation of business strategies. He found it consistent with his purpose to classify decisions as strategic, operative, and administrative. He also clearly distinguished subgoals and goal formulation, and finally arrived at a view of strategy formulation as a process in which the evaluation of synergistic $(2 + 2 = 5)$ effects played a dominating role. By seeking out opportunities which matched its strengths, a company could optimize the synergistic effects.

A similar view of strategy was presented in Katz (1970). Katz regarded corporate strategy as the relationship between an enterprise and its environment. He postulated two aspects of strategy: the *strategic posture* that refers to the actual relationship between the organization and its environment and the *strategic plan* that refers to intended future relationships. For a strategic plan to be workable, it should comprise scope, specifications, and deployments.

Katz defined *scope* in terms of markets and customers served, types of products, and basis of competition. By *specification* he meant some criteria that can be utilized for the description and evaluation of company performance. Desired objectives can also be established for each parameter and these objectives 'become a basis for planning the future activities of the enterprise'.

Ansoff's analysis strongly stressed the product–market mix and the opportunities for taking advantage of existing or potential synergies. Katz' *scope* could be expressed in the same terms as Ansoff's product–market mix, but Katz puts more emphasis on the rules of priority between different opportunities, and emphasizes the importance of explicit decisions on performance specifications. Further, Katz puts more emphasis than Ansoff on policies and timing.

Andrews (1971) has had a considerable impact on many researchers' and executives' ideas about corporate strategy. Andrews described corporate strategy as the pattern of major objectives, purposes or goals, and the principal policies and plans needed to achieve these goals. Andrews' view of corporate strategy is fairly close to Ansoff's and Katz's. However, he also argued that the personality of a company reflects aspects of its own and its management's intent that are only partly evident in a strategic plan. Andrews implies that strategic intentions cannot be fully expressed in clear-cut policy terms, and he adds that personal values, aspirations, and ideals influence a company's actions. Thus Andrews' approach to strategy and strategy formulation brings human beings into the picture.

In his later work Ansoff opposed his own earlier mechanistic views (as others also have done). The concept of 'strategic management' (Ansoff, 1978) was launched, implying that strategy formulation is in fact a continuous process in the organization. Instead of focusing so strongly on the elements of the strategy, the emphasis should be on discovering the structural properties that would promote organizational change and adaptation. And Ansoff also recognized that in order to understand the strategic process more fully, we need to know more about the mechanisms of organizational adaptation and change, and we need to examine such concepts as organizational norms, behavioural modes, leadership styles and organizational learning.

Organizational learning and development

Organization development (OD) emerged as an expanding field of theory and practice during the 1960s, in response to various problems connected with interpersonal relations and a perceived lack of creativity and low organizational adaptiveness. The underlying problem that called forth this response was to a great extent the same as that which had once generated the interest in strategy: can organizations be made to adapt more quickly and efficiently to a changing environment? But the definition of the problem, the level at which it was tackled, and the general methods used, were all quite different. The problems were mostly defined as psychological or social–psychological, and they were addressed at the group level or the individual level.

Beckhard (1969) defined organization development as 'an effort planned, organizationwide and managed from the top to increase organization effectiveness and health through planned interventions in the organization's processes using behavioural science knowledge' (p. 9).

Beckhard went on to describe how this definition of OD could be applied in areas such as team development, intergroup relations, goal-setting, planning and education.

Other researchers and practitioners focused more strongly on some specific method or set of problems. Schein (1969) focused on communication processes, functional roles in the group, group norms, and leadership. By making group members aware of the group processes during a 'process consultation', a series of observation and feedback sessions, Schein tried to make people more sensitive to what happened around them, which in turn should also make them capable of identifying, analysing, and solving whatever problems may arise.

Argyris (1964, 1970, 1976) and Argyris and Schön (1974, 1978) developed frameworks and models for penetrating and analysing those norms and behavioural modes in organizations that inhibit adaptation to a changing environment. Why do organizations so often fail to discover what is wrong with their current procedures, and why don't they find any really new ways of dealing with their problems? The answer, according to Argyris, lies in the existence of certain factors that inhibit organizational learning, that prevent organizations from discovering their errors and inventing new action strategies, from producing new behaviour and generalizing from what they have done. The inhibiting factors are particularly potent in the case of complex problems of organizational strategy and structure. These problems require learning of a more complex kind, learning that calls in question the fundamental norms on which present behaviour rests. Argyris calls this 'double loop learning' – as opposed to the more common single loop learning which proceeds like a thermostat, ensuring an equal temperature in a room. Thermostats do not question their own programs.

Subsequently, during the 1970s, growing concern has been expressed about the limitations of the various OD approaches. French and Bell (1978) call attention to the overemphasis on group dynamics and structure.

> 'Probably the most serious handicap of OD as it has emerged historically has been its overpreoccupation with the human and social dynamics of organizations to the detriment of attending to task, technical and structural aspects and their interdependencies ... In the future, organization development specialists must know much more about such matters as goal setting and structural changes and must

establish linkages with practitioners in such fields as management science, personnel and industrial psychology, operations research and industrial engineering in order to provide a broader range of options for organizational interventions.' (French and Bell, 1978; p. 257)

Schein expresses the same kind of views in the foreword to the Addison-Wesley series on organization development:

'Future volumes in the new series will explore the interconnections between OD and related areas which are becoming increasingly important to our total understanding of organizations, the process of management and the nature of work.' (Foreword by Schein in Beckhard and Harris, 1977; P. VII)

Some Basic Assumptions of IDS

Theories of strategy formulation and strategic management have thus been developed to cope with environmental change, which for most organizations is becoming both more complex and less predictable. But, the theories that have been developed (Ansoff, Katz, Andrews, and others) omit the most important component – the human being.

Theories of organizational learning and development have been evolved to cast some light on the way in which people in organizations develop norms to govern the way they work together. And yet these theories omit what are in fact the most important questions: How does the organization adapt, technically and structurally, to a changing environment? And how does it find a new business concept, new strategies and new programmes appropriate to new customer needs or new technologies?

So what we need is a theory of strategic management based on organizational learning and development. This theory must be behavioural in the sense that we start from what people actually do, and not from such abstract components as 'strategic posture' or 'level of uncertainty'. Such concepts may be useful later, but our point of departure must be the people in the organization.

The theory must also be concerned with the core problems of corporate and business strategies, policies, structure, and short-range planning. In short, the theory must integrate individual and group behaviour with technical questions of strategy and structure.

Let us therefore start with some broad assumptions (or axioms) about people and their organizational behaviour.

- People have theories or programmes which guide their actions, and which have evolved partly as a result of their experience in organizations.
- Certain theories or programmes are fundamental to our society, and these

appear long before the individual joins any organization for the purpose of work.

● People evolve programmes which they believe will be effective in fulfilling their physical, social, and other needs.

● People's individual programmes are only partially appropriate to collaboration in organizations. Some parts of the programmes have a destructive effect on organizational ends.

● People in organizations express themselves through strategies, policies etc.

● People will identify with strategies, policies etc. that they have espoused and become committed to.

These assumptions provide a basis for the following statements:

1. People in organizations create organizational 'strategies', 'policies', 'programmes', 'budgets', etc. These are sometimes highly 'technical' and sometimes on more of a 'commonsense' level, but they are always the result of human creation.
2. Organizational strategies, policies, programmes, and budgets constitute norms for behaviour in the organization.
3. People in organizations use the organizational language to express themselves. This language stems from the strategies, policies etc.
4. Strategies, policies etc. are expressed by people.

The loops thus developed may be constructive or destructive in relation to organizational effectiveness and to learning and development. The aim of all IDS work is to look into the nature of these loops, and to help the people involved to create constructive loops. This will include questioning strategies and policies, revising interpersonal behaviour, and, subsequently, inventing and acting through new and more constructive loops.

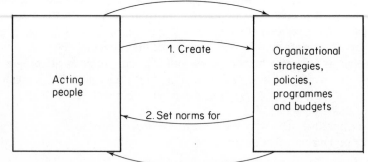

Figure 1.1. People and organizational control systems

Outline of the Book

The book consists of two parts and an epilogue. In the first part the theory of an integrated development strategy is presented. The second part presents two cases of IDS and a comparison between them. In the epilogue we discuss some of the complications of IDS in practice and discuss the importance it can have in the future.

In Chapter 2 we will discuss some development trends in the organizational environment and what impact these trends have on strategic thinking. We will argue that some new concepts are needed and we will present these in the 'strategy cycle'.

In Chapter 3 we will look more closely at the behavioural aspects of organizational learning and adaptation. We will discuss some of the factors that frequently prevent organizations from learning and discuss what measures could be taken to promote organizational learning.

Organizations often turn to consultants in order to get help in their development processes. Consultants intervene in the organizations in order to help. Intervention may also be undertaken by formal leaders within the system, or by internal change agents. In an integrated development strategy there are certain specific prerequisites for effective intervention. These will be analysed in Chapter 4.

In Chapter 5 we conclude the first part of the book by describing the integrated development strategy as a theory and a formal model for effective organizational adaptation and learning.

The second part of the book is devoted to case descriptions. Chapters 6 and 7 describe cases in which an intervention technique was used in working on an integrated development strategy.

In Chapter 6 the 'bypass theory of integration' is presented, and a case of strategy formulation and the implementation of business strategies in an organization is described. One of the present authors was involved in the case as a consultant.

In Chapter 7 the 'experiential theory of integration' is presented, and a case described in which the norms for relations between subsidiaries in a corporation are called in question and revised, and a new corporate strategy subsequently formulated.

In Chapter 8 we compare the two cases and analyse the practical implications of the two types of IDS. In this chapter the reader will find the principal differences in practice between a bypass and an experiential IDS. The book concludes with an epilogue.

CHAPTER 2

Environmental Change and Corporate Strategy

Some Changes in the Organizational Environment that Call for New Concepts of Corporate Strategy

During the 1980s organizations will be facing a new and challenging world. The picture is a complex and varied one: rapid technological and economic developments are taking place in many newly industrialized countries, and the balance of competitive advantage in the world is shifting; energy is becoming expensive and scarce rather than abundant and cheap; new power structures and behavioural modes are evolving in organizations, as values change and laws regarding equal opportunities and codetermination come into effect; people at all levels are becoming more prosperous and better educated and therefore less inclined to accept orders blindly and more prone to criticize hierarchical control; demand for goods and services is growing steadily less predictable and more dependent on evaluations made by a variety of organizations and institutions. In short, it is becoming increasingly difficult to lead and develop organizations successfully. Let us examine some of the main conditions of strategic thinking during the 1980s.

Industrial crisis accentuates the need for innovativeness

At the present time most industrialized countries, particularly in Europe, are going through a period of structural industrial crisis. Competition from new low-cost and low-price markets is a serious threat to many industries such as textiles and manufacturing. New and more economical iron ore deposits and new competitive conditions for the products of the forestry industry are depressing profits in the classical branches of industry in the developed countries. Energy prices are steadily increasing and causing new production problems, while rapid technological advances in such areas as electronics and biochemicals are generating structural changes in the competitive situation of most industries.

Thus it is no exaggeration to say that the industrialized countries are facing a new and in many ways more risky market situation. Much is required of companies in the way of flexibility, creativity, and market reorientation. But creativity, innovative ability, and new market thinking are not going to appear for the asking, like the genie in Aladdin's lamp. A great deal of open-minded and appropriately

12

designed development work is needed in order to encourage and increase innovative ability in companies. New marketing channels must be developed and new product concepts invented. Perhaps it is even more difficult to get rid of old products, production plants, methods, etc. than to invent something new. The resistance to change stems to a large extent from interests vested in the old ways of doing things; changing strategy becomes a question of organizational learning and development.

Democratic decision processes demand new organizational skills

All countries which are committed on principle to democracy, equality, and the freedom of the individual have to solve the problem of organizing for the realization of these values in practical everyday life. And since people spend most of their time in organizations, this is particularly important in organizational life.

Multi-interest working groups are generally designed to reflect as many facets of an organization as possible. In a business company each relevant employee category is usually represented by one member; different functional areas or hierarchical levels in the company will also be included, depending on the nature of the problem.

Because of the broad composition of the multi-interest groups, any differences in interest or outlook that exist in the company will be automatically accentuated in the group. The management culture will confront the grassroots, the white-collar will confront the blue-collar, production will come up against marketing and economics against technology. The more overriding and complex the problem to be tackled, the broader the representation, the greater the cultural differences.

The differences inherent in any group created specially to provide a broad approach to a problem may have the undesirable effect of reducing the efficiency of the individual members. Subgroups are formed, and these soon start vetoing one another on an 'I win, you lose' basis.

Any organization that hopes to succeed during the last two decades of our century must know how to plan for, and to implement, democracy at work; they must be able to carry projects through successfully in multi-interest groups and to cope with unions in a constructive dialogue.

Greater institutional interdependence calls for new dimensions in strategic thinking

Over the next two decades government regulations and national industrial policies are going to exert an increasing influence on business policies and strategies. Non-socialist politicians will of course continue to espouse the values of the free market system and to stress that industry should deal with its own problems. At the same time, however, the policies actually implemented will include measures to ensure the development of financial institutions for new industrial ventures and the protection of regions and towns from the misery caused by industrial restructuring; they will involve legislation to promote equal opportunities and industrial democracy and the regulation of prices to combat inflation; they will encourage development projects aimed at the export market, and so on. All such actions on the part of governments have one specific and unintended consequence: the mutual interdependence of government and industry will steadily increase, and this new situation will call for new concepts of strategic thinking in the business corporations.

Concentrated industrial structures make strategic planning more complex

Anti-trust laws may break up a few of the largest corporations, while investigations of competitive conditions may break up a few international trusts. But the general tendency during the 1980s and 1990s in practically every sector will almost certainly be a continued concentration of industry.

Airline companies will be larger and fewer; car manufacturers will meet the crisis by merging; the convenience goods sector is already dominated by a few multinational corporations, and a few distributors dominate operations in the individual countries. Due to the shifts in competitive conditions, the steel industry and other raw-material-based process industries have already been concentrated into large units which are increasingly controlled by national governments and cross-national organizations such as the Common Market. As these trends will probably persist over the coming decades, corporate planning will become increasingly complex. It will embrace bigger and more diversified companies; the interest groups connected with companies will become stronger and the values they represent will often conflict, and the companies themselves will comprise units working under widely varying market and environmental conditions.

Unions and interest groups must be dealt with in corporate strategies

The conflict between the privileged and the underprivileged will probably continue to grow: rich countries versus poor countries, rich people versus poor people, those who have jobs versus those who have not, well-paid workers versus low-income earners, and so on. It is no longer a clear-cut case of a conflict between capital-owners and wage-earners. The capital-owners are often institutions incorporating within themselves both private and public interests. And the various occupational categories are becoming increasingly aware that they are fighting one another for a finite supply of wage money. For the next ten years there will thus be an even greater area of conflict, in which the opposing interests of different categories of wage-earners, represented by large centralized unions, will confront one another. There will also be conflicts of interest between groups of capital-controlling institutions. Different regions and countries, each with their own natural resources and their demands for the largest possible share of the related wealth, will become increasingly aware of their interdependence and of the fact that they are often dealing with the same multinational corporations.

The typical corporation operates in several different regions and countries, embraces many categories of personnel, and uses money obtained from a wide variety of financial institutions. A major task for corporate management is thus to evolve strategies vis-à-vis all these groups with their conflicting values and interests. The task becomes yet more complex in view of the growing size of the corporations and the inherent conflict between the product level, the business level, the corporate level, and the industrial-sector level. In formulating its strategies management has to consider this great diversity of value groups and act in such a way as to bring dilemmas and ambiguities out into the open.

Technological development will compel companies to review their strategies

Recent developments in many technological fields have made it possible to produce old products in new ways. They are also generating new products and services that will alter, sometimes radically, consumer behaviour. This is particularly true in information technology and in biochemical research, to mention two of several important fields.

Let us take newspapers as an example, and see what the new information technology may mean. Newspapers result from a series of transformations of information from events to readers. First a journalist is somehow in touch with an event; by observing and interviewing he 'collects' the event and transforms it into a news item that he writes down. This is passed to an operator and reproduced as one component of a page. The page is cast as a plastic plate used in another department to print the actual newspaper. After some further processing, the newspapers are distributed to the readers.

There are several ways in which this production chain could be altered. Electronics could provide a radical change: a journalist would feed his page into a computer and the newspaper's subscribers could phone in to the computer and get the page on the TV screen; if they find it interesting they could have it printed on their own printers.

There are other ways, too, in which electronics and data processing could be used. The journalist could write directly into a computer that also controls one typesetting machine, and the paper could then be distributed as usual. Or the computer could control several typesetting machines for different regions or readerships.

The crucial questions are going to be: How are the newspapers going to use the new technology? What kind of products will replace the classic newspaper, or will the traditionally produced paper survive? And once a specific technological route has been decided upon, what timing will be appropriate?

The choice of technology mix, the use of technology in market segmentation and the timing of the introduction of new production technologies, will become an increasingly important variable in strategic decision-making.

International industrial relations will have an increasing impact also on national corporations

During the last thirty years we have learnt to classify the countries of the world according to certain criteria: East and West, communist and free world, poor and rich. Within these groups we also find specific subgroups. These stereotypes will probably become less relevant as the century nears its end. Poor countries may have oil; communist countries will be industrialized and will eventually become 'post-industrial'; religious and ethnic identity may be more important than either capitalism or communism.

Because of the changing character of many countries, the identification of friends and enemies, of partners, customers, or buying sources, may change dramatically. This will mean that during the next few decades there will be a shift in the patterns of trade and industrial structure. What was politically impossible or economically uninteresting in the 1970s may be politically feasible and economically interesting in the 1980s. And this in turn means that any Western companies which want to avoid the international threats and exploit the international opportunities arising from the shift in industrial structure and patterns of trade, must be prepared to look with fresh eyes at the whole question of multinational corporate strategy.

The Strategy Cycle

In order to cope with the kind of technical, social, and political development trends in the organizational environment that we have discussed above, we need to add to our traditional planning concepts. The new concepts should accord as far as possible with such organizational values and norms as are normally espoused by managements in developed countries, for example democracy, equal opportunities, decentralization, flexibility, development etc. We therefore suggest a strategy model based on the following considerations:

1. Strategy formulation and implementation should be regarded as an organizational learning process as described by the strategy cycle.
2. The initial phase of the cycle consists of the assessment of organizational and environmental uncertainty structures.
3. Organizational coping styles are analysed and one style is chosen as a consequence of what has been learnt about the type of uncertainty structures.
4. The value groups and interest groups that could influence the organization's success or failure are analysed, and a value-group strategy developed accordingly.
5. The freedom of choice as regards strategic decision variables is analysed: variables that can be decided unilaterally are separated from other decisions that have to be made jointly with one or more of the value groups.

6. Business and product–market strategies are formulated.
7. Organization and action plans are drawn up.

Strategy as a learning process

The effectiveness of a strategy will depend on:

1. how well the present organization–environment relation is understood;
2. how well future conditions are predicted;
3. the quality of the conclusions drawn from 1 and 2 in terms of strategic choice;
4. the efficiency with which strategic choices are translated into action; and
5. how the organization is adapted to the strategy.

Thus the effectiveness of a strategy will in fact depend on the ability of key people at various levels and in different functional areas to analyse and act together. The formulation and implementation of strategies should therefore be regarded as an organizational learning process: the actors concerned need to learn to identify, analyse, and act upon present and future attributes of their organization and its environment. This complex process can be illustrated as a 'strategy cycle' of the kind reproduced in Figure 2.1.

Time represents one dimension and level of abstraction another. The strategy cycle proceeds from the abstract analysis of organization and environment structures to concrete and specific action, and back again.

The assessment of uncertainty structures will result in the creation of a (new) organizational coping style. As a consequence of the further operationalization of the coping style, a value-group strategy is developed. It is necessary to identify the

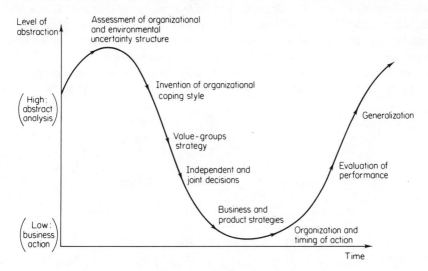

Figure 2.1. The strategy cycle

decisions that are independent of other value groups and those that must be made jointly. This will call for an even more concrete analysis, in which product and market strategies, financial policies, development plans etc. are decided upon. Finally, at the most concrete level of the strategy cycle, we find decisions about organization, timing, action plans and so on. The curve then returns to a more abstract level, as the evaluation of performance and the generalization of what has been learnt from previous actions takes over.

It should be remembered that the technical concepts of IDS discussed below will be useful in practice only when considered in conjunction with the behavioural processes to be explored later in Chapter 3.

Assessment of organizational and environmental uncertainty structures

Good resources, efficient administrative systems, and a dynamic organizational culture will enable an organization to cope with all kinds of environments, and will provide it with a wide range of alternative directions for development. An organization with inadequate resources, poor administrative systems, and a defensive organizational culture, on the other hand, will be very restricted in the choices it can make.

The worlds in which organizations operate can vary very much in their predictability, and uncertainty in the extraorganizational environment is thus a major determinant of the organization's freedom of action.

The value group, the market structure, and the stakeholder structure are all examples of possible sources of extraorganizational uncertainty. An organization whose stakeholders represent conflicting interests, whose markets are uncertain, and whose value groups pull in different directions, can be said to face a high degree of environmental uncertainty; an organization whose stakeholders are few and homogenous and whose markets and value groups are stable, on the other hand, has very little environmental uncertainty to grapple with.

The organization has diverse resources including equipment, competence, ideas, product development etc. These resources provide the organization with a

		Environment	
		uncertain	certain
Organization	uncertain	I Stressed	II Disturbed
	certain	III Dynamic	IV Dominant

Figure 2.2. A typology of uncertainty situations

secure base when it comes to coping with the environment. Another means of coping with the environment is through the control systems. The control systems and the resources together constitute the basis of organizational certainty (or uncertainty).

If we combine these two types of certainty and uncertainty, we can draw up the following typology of uncertainty situations (Figure 2.2).

This typology is based on a dichotomy of the variables which are used to define the organization's internal and external state of uncertainty. (For a detailed description of how to undertake such an assessment see Asplund, 1974.) The four types are defined below.

Type I: stressed situation

Organizations in this type of situation can be expected to have a low level of resources, fairly undeveloped administrative control systems, and little homogeneity in knowledge and values. These organizations face an uncertain environment, which means that they have a weak market position and are exposed to conflicting goals.

This situation is said to be stressed, because in the long run no organization can be expected to survive under such conditions. Organizations in this type of situation will have to develop their internal subsystems and change their environment in order to achieve a situation of type II or type III.

Type II: disturbed situation

Organizations in this type of situation operate in a secure environment; they have a strong market position and are not exposed to conflicting goals. On the other hand they have the same internal status as the first organizations, so that they perceive disturbances although their environment is in fact fairly stable. In the long run there is a risk that changes in the environment of type II organizations will cause them to revert to type I. To avoid this risk they must try to develop internal subsystems, which will ultimately make it possible for them to move on to type III.

Type III: dynamic situation

This type of situation is assumed to be an ideal type. The organizations operate in an uncertain environment, but because they do not experience internal uncertainty they can cope with the problems of uncertainty generated by the environment. But because of the high risk of falling into a stressed situation, the organization must be constantly on the alert to maintain its capacity to learn and develop.

Type IV: dominant situation

Organizations in this type of situation experience no uncertainty, and their main activity consists of controlling ongoing processes. However, in an increasingly complex and changeable environment, their product or market missions may quickly become obsolete. As the organizations do not face any environmental challenge, their internal certainty may easily degenerate, to be replaced by low morale, rigid bureaucracy, etc.

An analysis of the organization's uncertainty structure and a comparison between the organization and its main competitors will help to reveal the extent of its freedom of action and indicate the coping style that should be the most efficient.

Choice of organizational coping style

Let us look briefly at the coping styles attaching to the above typology, bearing in mind at the same time that the technical means discussed below must be considered in conjunction with the behavioural processes analysed in Chapter 3.

The stressed organization should focus on *short-term survival*. It is useless to speculate on possible long-term strategies, since the organization may well die in the immediate future unless some prompt action be taken. The critical uncertainty variables must be spotted, that is to say the cause of the stressed situation must be revealed. If resources are inadequate, certain cherished possessions may have to be sold to generate liquid funds or some new source of financing will have to be found. If the administrative systems are poor, extraordinary systems may have to be introduced to provide management as quickly as possible with the most valid and relevant short-run information.

In the longer term this is likely to be too crude and inadequate a control system, but for the moment the important thing is to create a short-run system adapted to the stressed situation.

It takes a long time to establish a good organizational culture, and it takes mutual trust and a sense of belonging to bring it to fruition. In the stressed situation all this may have to be laid aside. Some people may have to be removed. Some may be offered extra payments to stay and others to go. Personal commitment to the organization and effectiveness generated by self-actualization are not generally relevant at such a time. Instead coercion and commitment imposed by means of threats or promises may unfortunately be the only way to push a crisis programme through.

The stressed situation is also marked by external uncertainties. These may be removed by dropping certain products or markets, by getting rid of owners, by rejecting affiliation with certain value groups, etc. These negative decisions will not usually be popular or acclaimed; management will be blamed for being defensive, non-aggressive, and lacking in ideas for positive action; all of which means that the management concerned has to call on quite different skills than those which would be appropriate in a more 'normal' and prosperous organization. In IDS development work the focus on breaking behavioural deadlock must therefore be particularly strong.

In a *disturbed situation* profits may still be good and no external signs of inefficiency are apparent. The organization survives thanks to a benevolent and predictable environment. Development action in a disturbed corporation is often more difficult to motivate than in a stressed corporation. People are not aware that things are going wrong; that is in fact part of the problem. The corporation's situation is actually critical, since only a benevolent environment prevents a crisis. And yet there is no need for a crisis programme. A thorough-going development programme that focuses on the causes of the internal uncertainty is an appropriate way of coping with a disturbed situation. In an IDS this means that the organization has to be woken up. People must be confronted with well-supported facts showing the vulnerability of their situation.

The *dominant situation* may appear ideal: internally the situation is secure with adequate resources and control systems and an organizational culture that guarantees internal efficiency. The benevolent external situation further strengthens the organization. But the situation is not always as stable as it may seem. As the environment provides no challenge, the internal processes may eventually tend towards rigidity and bureaucracy. People may even start fighting one another, as they lack any external challenge or pressure. So the dominant organization may easily become disturbed if nothing is done to prevent such a development. The coping style appropriate to the dominant situation should focus on product and market development, thus eventually moving the organization into a dynamic situation. Behavioural development is also important if the organization is not to risk becoming an arena for internal conflict.

The *dynamic situation* is a more genuinely ideal type, and most strategy literature deals with the kind of organization—environment relationship that it involves. A competent organization makes a thorough analysis of its strengths and weaknesses in order to discover the opportunities in the environment that best match its own strengths and to uncover the threats to which it might be most vulnerable. We thus suggest that in this case the relevant literature provides helpful advice regarding growth, expansion, development, profit, or whatever objective is relevant. However, the models are not always properly understood or applied, because prevailing behavioural modes are such as to hamper problem-solving. Thus the traditional models will be more powerful if their users are simultaneously learning about behavioural norms and processes.

However, before we can decide what category an organization belongs to, a very thorough analysis will have to be made and a good deal of strategic learning undertaken.

Value-group strategy

Labour markets, capital markets, and all kinds of markets for goods and services are governed to a great extent by specific values and value groups (see Asplund, 1975). A labour union, for example, may constitute one such value group in competition or conflict with another union. Let us suppose that an organization depends on two categories of personnel, belonging to different unions. Let us further suppose that in view of certain market and cost developments, the organization has plans for introducing a new computer system that will reduce the number of employees from one or other of these unions. The system cannot be designed in a 'fair' way, spreading the reduction equally between the two. Each union will of course try to avoid their own members being affected. The organization is obviously in a difficult position, and it has to develop strategies for dealing with the two unions and possibly with other value groups as well, in order to handle the introduction of its computer system.

On the financing side the value groups are even more clearly defined and their internal competition more marked. Organizations are thus often limited to dealing with a single group. On the international level, however, or perhaps as a result of collaboration with other companies, it might be possible to avoid too strong a dependence on one specific value group in the financing field. But this will generally require a well thought out value-group strategy.

The principal media of exchange between an organization and its environment are money, products, and services. All such exchanges can be analysed in terms of markets.

According to classical microeconomic theory, price is determined by supply and demand. Modern 'regulators' (politicians, trusts, unions, or government economists) have reversed the causal order, declaring that supply and demand can be determined by regulating the price, or that price can be steered by determining total supply. As a result the organization faces a much more complex picture than is generally described in management literature. The markets are in fact often controlled by a great variety of institutions.

As we have seen, labour unions have a considerable say in the supply and the price of the services supplied by the individual to the organization; distributors, various consumer cooperatives, the public agencies for consumer affairs, purchase associations, and the media all help to decide what products will be exposed to the buyers, and what the final price and quality image will be. The financial institutions are controlled by the government, by political groups, and by other interest groups; they are therefore seldom neutral when it comes to furnishing organizations with financial resources.

In view of this highly institutionalized environment it seems to us that the concept of the *value group* is important to any analysis of the organization's transactions with its environment. A value group is defined as a group that exerts a fundamental influence on the supply, demand, price, financial conditions, and product image of a particular market or market segment. The organization will have to evolve specific relationships with a great many value groups, and these relationships will in turn determine the kind of market transactions that the organization will be able to enter into. In formulating a corporate strategy, the following are some of the questions that must be answered.

1. What value groups influence the selling or buying behaviour of various actual or potential markets?

2. How can the value groups influence market behaviour on these markets?
3. How can the organization cope with the specific value groups?

To summarize: the markets for products, services, labour, and capital, etc. are all controlled by value groups: value groups are thus an important factor with which an organizational strategy has to come to terms; value groups have to be identified, and their role and accessibility to action on the part of the firm analysed. As a consequence of this analysis a value-group strategy can be developed.

Independent and joint decisions

Strategy formulation is generally described as an activity undertaken in a top management group or at least in the upper echelons of the organizational hierarchy. This is only partially true. First, as we have already seen, several functions and several levels are involved in the strategy cycle. But more than this, strategic decision-making is not restricted to the one organization. In a great many cases we have found two essentially different kinds of strategic decisions: those that are taken unilaterally by the organization in response to developments in the environment, and those that are taken jointly in the sense that the organization and some other value group or groups are so dependent on one another that they decide to take joint, or at least highly coordinated, action. Sometimes joint decisions are even taken by competitors as a coordinated industry decision.

Business and product strategies

The general coping style that is chosen will affect the conditions for the organization's product and market strategy. If contraction is necessary, this will generally exclude many alternatives for product or market development that would have been attractive in a situation of dominance, for example. Thus the uncertainty structures in the organization and its environment will decide the general principles of calculation, the time horizon, and the conceptual models to be used in choosing products and markets.

Dominance would motivate the use of technical models such as Ansoff's product market synergy analysis for growth and expansion (see Ansoff, 1965). Dominance also motivates the launching of small 'entrepreneurial' projects with a high degree of uncertainty, or projects to open up the more stable elements in the environment. This means that various models of entrepreneurial management will also be applicable as supporting (technical) models in an IDS.

A *dynamic* type of organization–environment relationship will give scope for the application of models such as the Boston Consulting Group's portfolio model. Several works provide a survey of appropriate models and concepts for a dynamic situation (see in particular Hofer and Schendel. *Strategy Formulation – Analytical Concepts*, 1978). And as we have already seen, the dynamic organization–environment situation has been an implicit assumption in so many strategy models that there is no lack of documentation in this area of research. Thus an IDS interventionist will have quite a few well-documented models at his disposal in the technical areas, but these will have to be effectively integrated with a behavioural analysis.

The *stressed* situation calls for quite different kinds of product and market analysis. It is important here to recognize that the organization must create a more stable and predictable environment. This may mean that any product or market missions of a more demanding kind – very complex or wide-ranging perhaps – must be abandoned, even if they seem likely to bring in good profits in the future; the organization is simply not capable at present of bringing any complex projects to a successful conclusion. So even if a project is promising, and the organization appears to possess the requisite technical know-how, it will be better to abandon it, that is to say to sell it for cash now rather than in the future. Concentration and contraction call for models rather different from those normally described in textbooks and articles on strategy for growth and expansion. the integrated strategy will be particularly important here, since strategic learning in a stressed situation makes heavy demands on interpersonal behaviour.

The *disturbed* situation is characterized by stable external conditions but inadequate resources and systems. This kind of situation thus needs programmes appropriate to the internal issues; strategic development geared towards the environment will have to be pursued at a later date. Behavioural processes, in particular the development of norms, control systems, and interpersonal strategies, will generally be necessary before people even realize that something is actually wrong.

Organization and timing of action

In conventional thinking, organizational structure follows strategy formulation (see Chandler, 1962). We would argue that the development of strategy and structure should be regarded as interrelated, interdependent, and simultaneous processes. In order to get an organization to react adequately to the various elements in its own body and in its environment, it must organize itself in such a way as to facilitate learning. It must develop a capacity for reprogramming itself in light of what it learns both about itself and about conditions in its environment. Of course it is important to have organizational structures suited to the chosen coping style and the specific product–market mix. The point that we want to make, however, is that organizational structure should not be regarded as relevant solely to implementation. Rather should the reshaping of the organizational structure be seen as an integral part of the whole process of organizational learning. In the next chapter we can thus usefully turn to a closer examination of the behavioural conditions for organizational learning.

CHAPTER 3

Organizational Learning

Organizations Need to Learn

Organizations must learn in order to survive, to grow, and to prosper. As we discussed in Chapter 1, task and behaviour must be effectively integrated if an organization is to make full use of its human potential. And to make full use of human resources is vital to the development of effective strategies in an increasingly complex organizational environment.

But how do organizations learn and how do they learn to learn? Drawing on our experience we shall try to explore this question in the present chapter.

Individual and Organizational Learning

Most people have had the experience of learning a new skill as adults, whether it be some sport such as tennis, golf, or skiing, or a hobby such as photography or playing the guitar, or whether it be a new profession.

One of the problems connected with learning as adults is that we are already programmed: we have a 'natural' way of swinging a golf club, although it unfortunately only sends the ball 30 yards or so, that is if we hit the ball at all. So if we want to learn how to hit a golf ball we have, in a sense, to forget our 'natural golf swing' and start again from scratch. But can we in fact learn to forget our 'natural golf swing'? Probably not. It is impossible to unlearn a skill: we cannot learn not to be able to skate, not to ride a bicycle, or not to have our 'natural golf swing'. What we can do, however, is to learn additional or alternative programmes that will guide us in the execution of a skill. We can learn new ways of addressing the golf ball, holding the club, moving our bodies to prepare for a good swing, timing our movements when hitting the ball and following through.

But many a golfer recognizes the big gap between understanding the theory of the golf swing, and actually making a shot. We could even say that most golfers develop 'skills' consisting of doing things wrong. They produce the same slice or hook time and time again, although theoretically they know perfectly well how to make the 'perfect' shot. It is their 'natural swing', their initial programme, that will sneak out and ruin their performance.

From this example we can conclude that adult men and women have developed programmes in most areas of their lives; they have a 'natural' way of doing things. In order to learn a new skill they have to create new programmes that are more effective. And once having created a new programme they will have to find ways of getting it to steer their actions. Here the old 'natural' programmes operate chiefly as a threat to the new ones.

Let us consider these aspects of adult learning in an organizational context. As members of the organization people have learnt how to do certain things: how to market products, make forecasts, manage departments, or carry out any of the other necessary technical tasks. They have also learnt how to earn rewards and avoid punishments. Top executives have learnt how to win against competitors and how to promote their own careers; they have learnt how to master other people who have coveted their positions, and they have learnt how to acquire supporters for their own protection. Not all learning that takes place in the organization will necessarily promote organizational effectiveness. Executives have also learnt how to cover up errors, how to form secret groupings, how to threaten subordinates or competitors, and how to get subordinates to conform. Similarly subordinates have learnt how to conform, how to report the things they believe the boss wants to hear, and so on. In the technical area, too, people have learnt ways of doing things that may not be productive of present or future efficiency. They may have learnt marketing methods that no longer fit modern market conditions, or methods of production based on outdated technological knowledge. Thus some of the programmes learnt by organization members are inadequate for achieving organizational goals. They lead to the conservation of the status quo, or even to the spread of organizational dry rot.

If an organization is to become more effective, its members must develop programmes to include the production of valid and relevant information and to promote restructuring within or between groups. At the same time the programme must be consistent with the calls of organizational adaptation and development.

Organizational learning finds expression at the organization (rather than the individual) level: the organization 'learns' to develop new products, new markets, new production and marketing methods, or whatever is needed in order to survive and prosper in the relevant environment. But all this is the result of a learning process at the personal and interpersonal level. Thus any attempt to promote a learning process intended to produce new strategies or new organizational policies, must address itself to people: people are going to have to develop new programmes for dealing with one another and with the various technical problems; and these people must be given the opportunity to try out the new programmes in practice, they must learn to become skilful in new types of interpersonal and technical behaviour.

Learning about the Organizational Culture

Learning about the organizational culture implies learning about:

1. the norms and control systems that have been built up in the organization for the fulfilment of its tasks; and

2. the programmes evolved by individual organization members to promote their own survival and success in the organization.

It also means learning how to change ineffective norms, control systems, or personal programmes.

Norms and control systems

The norms of an organization may prescribe the taking of chances, thinking ahead, and sounding the alarm about competitive threats; or they may encourage everyone to keep quiet about unpleasant things. The norms may favour open and courageous behaviour towards people in power, or they may advocate treating powerful people with the greatest respect. The norms of the organization, whatever they may be, will have become firmly rooted in the people working there.

The norms of the organization are reflected in the various control systems functioning there, in the hierarchy, the reward systems, and the formal planning and control systems. Not only are the norms manifest in these control systems, they are in turn reinforced by them (see Figure 3.1).

If the prevailing norms are favourable to change, development, and learning, these positive characteristics will show in the design of the control systems, and the control systems themselves will then further strengthen the positive norms. Unfortunately, however, the prevailing norms are often such as to inhibit learning and development.

Ineffective norms are unfortunately all too common in organizations. People may have discovered that it does not pay to report negative deviations from a plan, for instance, especially if the deviation is due to an error in judgement higher up the hierarchy; and so the discovery of weaknesses in organizational performance is unnecessarily delayed (for a more detailed analysis of ineffective norms see also, e.g., Argyris, 1976).

To criticize someone openly is often held to be impolite; it is better to protect the offender from hearing anything negative about himself, and to solve the problems without involving the person who has made the errors.

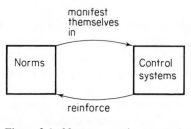

Figure 3.1. Norms and control systems

Taking risks involves a fair chance of losing. In many organizations people are severely punished for taking risks that do not succeed. They may be given only one chance, and in that kind of situation it is often better to play safe. If you never take any chances, you will never lose – on the other hand, of course, there's not much chance of winning either. The result of such a conservative attitude is often that no new products are tested, no new markets are tackled, and no new methods of production or marketing are tried out.

People who win battles, who can control those around them, and who can take a punch on the head and bounce back again are normally regarded as strong and dependable members of any organization. They are the ones to be trusted as leaders. This way of evaluating people gives rise to a special set of norms: never show weakness, never admit defeat even if you are wrong, never become emotional, and always bounce back after a blow. People working under the shadow of a value and norm system like this will tend to withhold information in order to have an extra card up their sleeves, they will seek out spectacular battles that they know they can win, and they will operate secret strategies against one another.

In an organizational setting in which people are defensive, conservative and apt to exert control, it will not be possible to evolve a free and relaxed way of exchanging information or working constructively together to solve any problems that come up. People will be too afraid, too cautious, to confront one another openly, and so the secret win-or-lose games continually undermine the organizational culture.

The presence of such defensive and conservative norms in the culture will be reflected in the control systems. Planning will focus on the detection of errors and deviations, but will allow sufficient margins for cover-up. If people feel that they are not trusted, and that others higher up are trying to control them, they will look for ways of beating the control system. A great deal of time will be spent working out how to report 'upwards' in such a way as to conceal the mistakes or negligence committed, and much less energy will be devoted by individual employees to doing a good job to the best of their ability.

The hierarchical control system, the planning system, and the systems for following up results will thus all reflect the underlying organizational norms. And once the norms are truly embedded in the organizational systems, they become much harder to shift.

But in some organizations effective norms do in fact evolve. Perhaps people feel so much personal commitment to the organizational goals, to the production technology, or to collective organizational success, that the positive forces thus generated are stronger than the negative pulls described earlier. Or positive norms may have evolved as a result of competent management. If people feel trusted, they generally try to do better than if they feel mistrusted; if they are informed openly of their errors, and if a reasonable amount of error is permitted, they will react by being more open themselves, ready to admit to errors, and prepared to rectify them; if they are allowed their ups and downs and are evaluated on their average performance, they will feel fairly treated and will themselves act fairly in terms of organizational ends. If risk-taking is promoted by top management, other people too will be prepared to take some risks so long as they know they won't be shot if they don't always succeed.

This pattern of management action and organizational reaction will generate norms that are positive to organizational growth and survival. One of the basic objectives in any company hoping to promote organizational learning is thus to create a norm system that permits the generation and free exchange of information. The norms and the control systems then constitute an important element in organizational learning.

Individual programmes

At a certain level of abstraction we can say that the people in the organization behave according to specific norms. If we go down to a more individual level, we will see that the way people behave in particular situations may vary considerably, although still bounded by a particular norm system. One person may be afraid of losing his position, another is struggling to improve his position, yet another has given up his professional ambitions, while another regards formal positions of power as unimportant. Individual attitudes of this sort will greatly affect the programmes that the various members develop and pursue in order to achieve their own personal goals in the organization. Personality characteristics, previous experience, and financial dependence on the job are all examples of factors that can help to explain why people evolve their own particular programmes for coping with reality.

The personal programmes evolved for dealing with various kinds of situation will vary in their effectiveness, in terms of both personal and organizational goals. In developing a capacity for ogranizational learning and adaptation, it will therefore be necessary to focus both on the organizational norms and control systems *and* on the personal programmes of the key groups in the organization. In both we may find strong factors that inhibit organizational learning.

Making the Unmentionable Mentionable – What We Say and What We Do

There are often big inconsistencies between what people say they do, and what they actually do. Sometimes people are aware of these inconsistencies, but believe they are the only ones to have seen through them. But more often people are not even aware of any difference between what they say and what other people 'hear' in what they say. The top executive of a large corporation, for example, was always making speeches about the importance of decentralization and of enhancing the conditions for creativity and initiative at lower levels in his organization. At the same time, however, he was busy launching a more centrally controlled budget procedure to stop waste at lower levels. He was also introducing a new cash-management programme, whereby money was entirely controlled by the central financial unit, and he was initiating a standardized and mechanistic strategy-formulation programme, run by experts from a large American consulting firm. In short, while loudly espousing the values of decentralization, creativity, initiative, and entrepreneurship, he was acting firmly to increase central control and restrict freedom of action at lower levels. People at lower levels were not blind to this fact; neither was the chief executive. But what he failed to understand was that he was creating an atmosphere of mistrust and secretiveness. Eventually things went noticeably wrong with the company, and its chief executive was removed. But sometimes mistrust and a poor organizational climate can prevail for a long time before any concrete results in the shape of falling profits and an unsound economy actually appear. In the meantime the innovativeness and strategic alertness of the organization will have been deteriorating steadily.

The discrepancies between people's 'espoused theories of action' and their 'theories in use' have been examined and analysed by Argyris and Schön (1974). One of Argyris' conclusions is that if an individual wants to develop a more effective type of behaviour, he must become aware of the discrepancies between his own espoused theories and his theories in use, and he must strive to minimize the gap. In our experience the discrepancies between espoused theories and theories in use are equally prevalent and equally dysfunctional in both the technical and the behavioural areas. And the concepts are as relevant on the organizational level of analysis as they are on the interpersonal level. We can usefully extend the range of the concepts and speak of an *espoused corporate strategy* and a *corporate strategy in use* or an *espoused organizational power structure* and a *power structure in use*.

Behavioural norms (and taboos) are lodged in the people who constitute the organization. Thus, no matter what the official or espoused norms may prescribe, people will behave according to the organizational norms *in use*, that is to say according to the norms applied by the people around them in the organization. Also, we must not forget that people in organizations act by performing *tasks*, as well as by the acts traditionally regarded as constituting (social) behaviour. This means that there is not really any dividing line between task processes and behavioural processes. None the less a dividing line has been drawn up (for theoretical purposes), but in our view it acts as a major obstacle to both individual and organizational learning and development. The greater the gap between an individual's espoused theories and his theories in use, the more likely it is that the organization in which he operates has norms that violate and/or contradict one another.

Consider the following example. A large motor-car manufacturing company is expecting demand for its private cars to fall off during the 1980s. Competition on the private car market is becoming keener and something has to be done. The truck division seems to offer the most promising product line for the 1980s. One possible strategic action would be to cease production of private cars and to expand trucks and other promising products. However, open discussion between divisions about the failure and problems of one of them is not consistent with the norm decreeing that every division operates as an autonomous unit except on questions of finance. Another strong norm discourages negative thinking. Hence old mistakes in forecasting and product choice were never openly discussed; but everybody secretly blamed the managing director for the mistakes, although he was never openly confronted with any criticism by his colleagues or by the divisional managers.

Thus although there was a strongly espoused norm of high risk-taking and creativity in this company, people were in fact afraid of openly examining the possibility of a change in strategy, since this would have meant violating several strong (tacit) norms, such as: 'Never bring up old mistakes, what is done is done', or 'Stick to your own business and don't get mixed up in the problems of other divisions', or 'Don't let the Managing Director know about other people's mistakes', or 'See that your own mistakes are covered up'. These norms left responsible middle managers feeling afraid to question certain earlier production decisions; as a result they could not really understand everything that was happening in the private-car world and were consequently unable to be creative or to contribute anything to discussions on future strategy.

Another kind of conflicting norm that we have often come across in Swedish organizations has resulted from the new laws on industrial democracy which have often remained at the level of espoused theories. According to the Co-determination Act most companies are required to include a trade union representative at meetings of the Board. Naturally the Board is obliged to conform to the law, and it cannot of course prevent the union representative from sharing all the information on which its decisions are based. To counteract the effects of this, however, a great many informal meetings and much lobbying now take place. The company has to espouse the norm that prescribes supplying full information to the union members, but in fact many important questions are either delegated to a management level where less 'democratic' procedures prevail, or they are discussed outside the board room. The unions realize this but often consider it more efficient to develop secret strategies of their own than to discuss the problem openly. So instead of coming out in the open and taking up the principle with management, the unions 'try to push questions further up the line', hoping they will finally get to board level, even though they realize that some of the questions could be solved more easily at other levels. Another secret strategy that the unions sometimes use is to stop other projects in order to improve their bargaining position. These tendencies can be identified at all hierarchical levels, and we have often found that at the lower levels both the union representatives and the line managers dislike these norms that force them to behave dysfunctionally; they are not always fully aware of the cause and effect, and if they are, they do not feel free to come out into the open and start questioning company and union strategies.

These examples may suffice to illustrate how the discrepancies between espoused norms and norms in use (or espoused strategy and strategy in use) have dysfunctional effects on the efficiency of operations and strategy formulation. Certain questions become unmentionable, so that dialogue in the organization remains superficial and incapable of generating much organizational learning. Consequently the organization's ability to adapt to changing conditions deteriorates.

In view of all this, what we need are ways of making the unmentionable mentionable and the invisible visible. And to achieve this we will have to work for a closer integration between technical areas such as product development, strategy formulation, and information-systems development on the one hand, and the creation of more functional behavioural norms – greater openness, trust, and risk-taking etc. – on the other. Only when people from different departments, from unions and management, or from different divisions, can face one another openly and confront one another with the real problems, will we have a chance to create conditions favourable to organizational learning.

The Concepts of Key Groups

The problem at the core of organization theory has always been how to organize people effectively in order to accomplish a particular task. In attempting to solve this problem, organization theory has come to embrace a variety of increasingly sophisticated and elaborate theories of the organization. In some of these the stress is on structural problems, in others it is on problems of development and growth.

Some of the more recent theories of organizational behaviour focus on the irrationalities of the decision-making processes and on the ad hoc nature of the ideal structure (contingency theory). Systems thinking has also had an important impact on the perception of organizational effectiveness. The overall model provided by systems theory constitutes a good basis for explaining the interaction processes between an organization and its environment. It can therefore also provide a point of departure for our analysis. An organization can be regarded as a system engaged in a continual process of resource exchange between itself and its environment. Various groups in the organization system are involved in the processing of resources to produce some good or some service that will be evaluated by the environment. Some of the groups have more power (be it formal or informal) than others, and we can designate these *key groups*. From a strategic point of view the role of the key group is twofold:

1. a key group must be able to foresee and correctly identify changes in the system's environment; and
2. a key group must be able to identify the people (or groups) in the system who can engender change.

Identifying key groups

In organization and leadership theory much has been written about the formal and informal aspects of power and authority. It is widely agreed that the picture presented by the organizational chart does not altogether tally with the (real) day-to-day activities of the organization. However, we can assume that the men and women at the top of an organization constitute a key group. Naturally, though, there may be more than one key group which influences both the present and the future state of the organization; in fact, one of the most important tasks of the key group that is formally at the 'top' is to identify other existing or potential key groups which constitute part of a flexible organization's preparedness for change.

According to this view management's strategic role can therefore be said to include:

1. foreseeing various differences in the evaluations to which the output of their organization may be subjected;
2. identifying (potential) key groups connected with pressures stemming from these differences; and
3. generating or promoting the kind of structural actions and processes that are likely to encourage the birth and facilitate the performance of such 'new' key groups.

This last task is a very difficult and delicate one. Few of the theories concerned with business policy and strategy formulation even touch upon it, probably because human beings and their social behaviour are not allowed for in the models. In a purely rational world (from the organization's point of view), people in positions of power could be made responsible for retiring voluntarily from the scene of action as soon as they realized that they were harming or endangering the future of their organization. But human beings are not totally rational from the organization's point of view, which means that they are liable to react emotionally, or rationally from the personal point of view, whenever their power is threatened.

So instead of encouraging and facilitating the birth of new key groups or the adoption of new key group members, the present key group will often counteract any activities that might result in a change in the power distribution of the organization. If we are right in this assumption, then we are faced with some serious dilemmas.

How can the members of a key group be expected to encourage others to learn and explore fears and anxieties, when they are not themselves prepared to do so? And how can the members of a key group face up to these dilemmas in the group itself, when the very glue that holds the group together is its position of power vis-à-vis other competing groups?

One obvious conclusion is that any development work intended to include the questioning of fundamental values or organizational strategies, must start at the very top of the organization's hierarchy. Another conclusion is that successful development work must involve all the major key groups in the organization.

An Organizational–Behavioural Learning Cycle

Organizational learning means that an organization correctly identifies developments in its environment and that it develops its own capacity to deal effectively with this environment. This kind of learning consists of several steps, in which different organizational actors play the dominating roles. As different people in the organization are involved, organizational learning also means that people learn not only how to deal with changes in the environment but also how to deal effectively with one another. Let us forget for the moment those aspects of organizational learning that we have already discussed in Chapter 2 in connection with the strategy cycle, and focus here on the behavioural aspects of organizational learning instead.

As a first step it will be necessary to examine and analyse the organization's culture: norms and control systems may be functional or dysfunctional to organizational goals; espoused strategies and objectives or norms may differ greatly from those actually in use; and the wrong people or the wrong groups may be involved in fundamental organizational processes. We can call this process of making organizational discoveries the 'assessment of organizational culture'.

However, the organization will not change just because people have become more aware. New norms must be created and launched, and new control systems established (or old ones changed) in such a way that people will identify with the new norms not only by espousing them but also by putting them into practice.

This might mean, for instance, that the establishment of new relations between head office and subsidiary companies must be accompanied by changes in control systems (perhaps a new system of reporting and new ways of handling investments) which give credibility and substance to the new norms underlying the altered arrangements. Only then will it be meaningful to work with individual actors and their personal action strategies. This argument can be illustrated by the same kind of figure that we used in Chapter 2 to describe the strategy cycle. The cyclical movement from the abstract level of analysis to the concrete level of action is the same, but the focus of attention has changed. Here we are concerned with learning about the behavioural aspects of the organization's activities, whereas in Chapter 2 we focused on the technical, strategic aspects of organizational learning and adaptation. The behavioural–organizational learning cycle is illustrated in Figure 3.2 below.

The two cycles illustrated here and in Chapter 2 are obviously very closely interrelated. If people have not learnt how to deal with one another, they will not be effective when they try to solve technical problems together. And similarly, an apparently favourable organizational culture will not be much use unless it is geared towards technical learning about the organization and its environment.

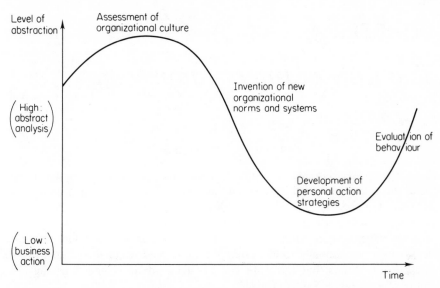

Figure 3.2. A behavioural–organizational learning cycle

We will return to the question of how to integrate these learning cycles in Chapter 5. First, however, let us focus on the question of intervention and consultative activities that will help to promote effective organizational learning.

CHAPTER 4

The Role of Intervention

The Roles of Consultants

As we have seen in the previous chapters, the processes of strategic and behavioural organizational learning are not easy. Much courage and many skills are needed in order to acquire the kind of knowledge relevant to an understanding of organizational environments and the human dynamics of organizations.

It has therefore become almost a necessity for companies embarking on major development programmes to hire external help. Large organizations often engage internal consultants, but there are good grounds for recommending that consultants be brought in from outside:

- The external consultant is not blinded by familiarity. At least to begin with he or she is free of organizational preconceptions and can therefore help the organization to look at itself and its problems through different coloured spectacles.
- The external consultant has experience of many different organizations and can act as a kind of translator between researchers and practitioners.
- On account of his external and temporary engagement, the consultant can view things in a longer perspective.

However, as we saw in the previous chapter, there are a great many factors which can hamper organizational learning and, because consultation is a process involving two parties, the client and the consultant, the consultant may not always be able to overcome these obstacles. Expectations, perceived roles, and motives simply may not match.

In much of the growing literature that deals with consultancy and consultant roles, consultants are regarded as doctors, teachers, or mediators. Below we will discuss the widely accepted doctor–patient model and some of its dilemmas. But first we ask our readers to consider a client–consultant relationship in which the client, although he has turned to a consultant with the declared intention of learning, does not in fact intend to learn at all. The client may say, for instance, 'I want to learn how to solve this', but what he is really thinking is, 'I want you to do this (for me)', and he probably has in mind certain very specific tasks such as the following:

- *Justifying old decisions*: the consultant assumes the role of *hostage* or

36

witness, someone who can argue eloquently to show how things have improved as a result of certain former decisions.

● *Making 'objective' evaluations* of errors committed by the former administration. The consultant assumes the role of *truth possessor*, who furnishes top management with motives for making unpopular decisions or getting rid of disloyal people.

● *Getting feedback from lower levels*; here the consultant assumes the roles of *spy* or *court jester*.

● *Creating a positive image of management*; the consultant may have to convince various parties inside or outside the organization that management is progressive and modern, that it really is in favour of development. Here the consultant assumes the role of *alibi*.

● *Carrying out some difficult and unpopular tasks*; the consultant assumes the role of *hired gun*.

It may take some time before the consultant becomes aware of the roles he may actually be playing. In some cases both consultant and client may well be perfectly happy with these roles: the client gets his job done and the consultant is paid for doing it. But many consultants are trapped in a dysfunctional role before they realize it, and may then find it almost impossible to throw it off – once a jester always a jester. But if the consultant's role is that of hostage, witness, truth possessor, spy, jester, alibi or gun, effective organizational learning is not going to result.

We mentioned earlier that the most common and recognized role for the consultant is that of the 'doctor'. But even this role has its problems, and it is therefore appropriate now to examine some of the characteristics and the impact on learning of a doctor–patient model of consultation.

Some Consequences of the Doctor–Patient Model of Consultation

In analysing the doctor–patient model, Schein (1969) found one of the fundamental shortcomings of the model to be that responsibility for the diagnosis was left entirely to the 'doctor'. Schein's solution was to modify the role of the consultant, whose prime responsibility he declared to be 'to help the client to perceive, understand and act'. But in Schein's model of process consultation the doctor–patient relationship still persists to a great extent, although the doctor has become a psychoanalyst instead of the more traditional physician. Thus it seems necessary to go one step further in the critique of the doctor–patient model, and to develop an alternative design.

There are at least three conditions on which the doctor–patient model relies, namely:

1. a relatively clear picture of the client and of the patient;
2. a relatively clearly delimited problem; and

Table 4.1. Consultant Client roles in the doctor–patient model

Problem	Responsible actor
1. Perceived symptoms	client
2. Tender, contract	client (consultant)
3. Diagnosis of Problem	consultant
4. Recommended action	consultant
5. Implementation of action	client (consultant)
6 Follow-up action	client (consultant)

3. a battery of tested methods and techniques (remedies).

The first two of these promote a quick and efficient diagnosis of the 'fault', and the third makes possible an assured prescription of the measures required for a cure.

However, the situation in a real-life present-day organization no longer provides these conditions. It is not easy to isolate problems or to single out organization members. There are many reasons for this. Sociocultural factors have played their part, in particular a new awareness of the social consequences of company action. Major changes in the decision structure of organizations – the growing importance of project groups, a greater measure of employee participation in major decisions, the spread of joint consultation councils – have also altered the picture, and so has the extended time horizon attaching to many decisions today. Furthermore, different groups and different levels in organizations are more dependent on one another than they used to be, and it is no longer efficient to develop partial solutions; indeed, from the point of view of organizational policy, it is unwise.

The harsh economic climate which most companies are now experiencing makes it necessary to seek solutions that will be efficient over a relatively long term. Companies cannot afford to experiment with purely short-term solutions; all such efforts must be regarded as an investment in improving the company's own built-in competence, so that it will be possible to cope with similar problems in the future without having to call in help from outside.

Traditional intervention in accordance with the doctor–patient model of consultation can be described in the following steps (see Table 4.1).

The process in Table 4.1 reveals many similarities with the traditional decision process; but here the action and the responsibility at the different stages attach sometimes to the client and sometimes to the consultant. The client is more active in phases 1, 2, 5, and 6 and the consultant in phases 3 and 4. Phase 1 generates

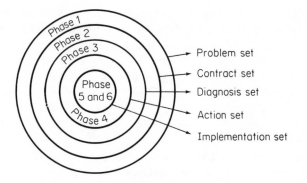

Figure 4.1. Consultant–client sets

phase 2; phase 2 fixes phase 3 and phase 3 determines phase 4; after which the organization (the client) reassumes power and decides whether or not to proceed to phases 5 and 6.

We can also see the phases as a successive delimitation of potential sets, which leads us finally into the inner circle as illustrated in Figure 4.1.

The consultant and the client work their way towards the circle alternatively, assuming in turns the responsibility and freedom to design the next phase. The main meta-values of the doctor–patient model are:

1. the rational and resource-saving distribution of roles and responsibility during the process of consultation;
2. consultant responsibility for diagnosis and feedback of the diagnosis result to the client;
3. approval of the contract between client and consultant at the beginning of the project;
4. client responsibility for implementing possible changes once the assignment is complete and has been reported.

The consultant who is an expert in his field will normally be the one responsible for the validity of the technical solution, but he will leave to the client the main responsibility for learning how to apply the technical solution. Furthermore, since the client has little if any knowledge of the process by which the consultant arrived at a particular solution, it is difficult for the client to do anything other than totally accept or totally reject 'the solution'.

Some common values among consultants

To a consultant supporting himself entirely on the proceeds of his consultancy assignments, it is often of vital importance to acquire and retain an ever-increasing number of assignments. The more assignments he has and the larger they are, the greater will be his resulting social prestige and other benefits.

It is often possible for consultants to earn a reputation for success by getting their solutions – probably the transfer or firing of one or more top people in the client company – accepted. As a result of this worldly evaluation of consultancy, consultants often regard 'winning' over the client as an important value that governs their approach to their work. Most consultants would say that to carry an assignment through effectively, they must be allowed as far as possible to influence its goals. Ideally the consultant likes to be able to define the task himself. A major value is therefore to define, and subsequently to achieve, the goals of the assignment himself.

These values generate certain specific consulting strategies, which in turn will have certain implications for learning and efficiency.

Common consulting strategies

It becomes a major part of the consultant's strategy to acquire for himself control over and 'possession' of the assignment. This means that he tries to design situations which he can control. (Residential conferences and courses can provide an appropriate tool here.) And the inclusion of several consultants responsible for different parts of the project will increase the strength of the consultant team. The consultants can then develop norms among themselves, confirming their right to 'own' and control the assignment.

Another way of reinforcing their 'ownership' of the different jobs is to develop investigatory and analytical tools with which they alone are familiar, and over which they alone have control. When the consultant feeds back information to the client, he can then do it in such a way that the client has no chance of testing the validity of the information he receives. The client will have to base his acceptance or rejection of the consultant's conclusions on a general evaluation of the reputation of the consultant and the reliability of his analysis.

By taking personal responsibility for the success or failure of running the project, the consultant reinforces his possession of and control over the assignment. This strategy is often shored up by the client, who is only too happy to be able to blame the consultant if anything goes wrong. Because of his uncertain position in relation to his client, the consultant often feels safer bearing direct responsibility and acting as prime mover in the project.

Once the consultant has taken steps to possess and control the assignment, and has assumed responsibility for its success, it is only logical that he should try to appear as the strong and rational man of action. The client has often pushed most of the responsibility on to the consultant, whom he will therefore have to trust without altogether understanding what he is doing. The consultant will naturally try to encourage this confidence by showing himself to be strong and rational and competent in all situations, and by never admitting to the weaknesses or inadequacies that in fact he may possess.

A useful tactic for the consultant who wants to avoid being questioned is to refer to higher levels in the company or to some vague authority – 'research', perhaps, or 'my long experience' – in such a way that the client cannot ask any questions without appearing ignorant. The consultant thus strengthens his own position, accrediting his analyses and solutions by reference to authoritative sources whose relevance or reliability the client has no chance of checking. The client is thus trapped; the consultant has every chance of retaining and extending the assignment and of defeating any potential opposition to his analyses or solutions.

Another important means of control is the acquisition of the 'right' allies in the organization, preferably from several different centres of power. The possibility of being able to play people off against one another, or at least to hint at such a possibility, can greatly affect the consultant's chances of 'winning'. As well as establishing contact with the obvious centres of power the consultant can also form coalitions at a lower level, with the workforce (of which the various bosses are often afraid). After all, a boss speaks 'upwards' as the representative of his team; if the consultant succeeds in making good contact with this team, the boss may feel threatened. If the consultant also manages to establish himself 'upwards' – with the boss's own boss – he will be able to reinforce his position continually by playing off different levels, which often lack mutual points of contact, against one another. All this gives him an excellent chance of winning any 'games' that occur, or even of initiating games that he knows perfectly well he can win. But, most important of all, he will probably be able to retain the assignment, and possibly even have it extended.

The consultant who succeeds in pursuing action strategies of the type described above will often be regarded as successful by his colleagues and clients. But by his very success in obtaining and retaining and extending his assignments, in winning rather than losing, and in defining the assignments on his own terms, he has lost much of what could have made his intervention effective. The consultant's own behaviour has become calculating and manipulative, and the consultant–client relationship has turned into a power game. Just as the consultant evolves strategies for gaining victories over the client, so the client designs others to help him to win points off the consultant. These strategies must be secret in order to succeed, and this very secrecy often means that one party fails to understand the reasons for the other's behaviour. Misunderstandings arise, reinforcing the already defensive and manipulative norms that have been evolving.

Since the diagnoses and recommendations presented to the client are based on models and data of which he is ignorant, he will not be able to analyse and test the advice he receives from the consultant. He will accept or reject the recommendations on other grounds: because of the general confidence he feels in the consultant, or because the solutions agree with his own preconceived ideas.

Learning effects

Any learning that takes place as the result of a traditional expert consultation will probably be restricted to the case at hand, the case for which the consultant has designed his diagnostic methods and made his prescriptions. In fact, because of his active driving role and his 'ownership' of the assignment, the consultant is really the only one who is likely to achieve any discernment or any generalized learning as a result of what has been done.

If any other problems arise in future, the client will still have to depend on the support of a consultant. He has admittedly been helped with one particular problem, and the consultant's solution and recommendations may be extremely good. But the client has not been helped to solve problems so that they remain solved; he has not learnt how to learn from his own experience, or how to analyse and handle his own situation constructively.

An IDS Consultation Process

Objectives

The two main objectives of an IDS consulting process are to create conditions for learning and to focus on both task and behaviour.

The *focus on learning* is important as it is only through learning that an organization can recognize, analyse, and act upon new events within its own body or in its environment. But how does a consultant create conditions favourable to organizational learning? A first necessary condition is the generation of valid and reliable data. Another condition is that the process permits the free exchange of all relevant data and evaluations. This means that organizational taboos, veto processes, and defensive organizational norms must be brought out into the open and changed or, failing that, that the interventionist must find ways of overcoming the power of these inhibiting forces.

The *integration of task and behaviour* is the other major objective of an IDS intervention. This approach makes very special demands on the interventionist and on his handling of the intervention process. First the interventionist must be a genuine expert in the relevant task area. If he is an expert on marketing, for instance, it will be a much more difficult job for him to demonstrate openly to the client the way in which he proposes to analyse a problem than it would be to perform an analysis secretly and in private, and then to make his recommendations accordingly. The interventionist must have such a good command of his field of knowledge that he can stand up to an open confrontation. His models and methods must be so valid and reliable that they can bear the close scrutiny of the client. Further, the interventionist must be able to suggest alternative models and methods, and be able to explain to the client the advantages and disadvantages of the different techniques.

In an IDS intervention the consultant must also command behavioural science methods and techniques with sufficient confidence to be able to transmit behavioural learning to the client. This is even more difficult in an IDS project than in an ordinary behavioural intervention, as the consultant himself plays an active role in the analysis of the task. However, it is feasible if the intervention is organized on lines other than those usually followed, and if the consultant is open to confrontation.

Strategies to create an IDS intervention

1. The *integration of learning cycles* is the fundamental consultation strategy in an IDS intervention process. The consultant collects behavioural data such as intergroup communications, openly espoused values at the top etc., and feeds them back in an elaborated form. At the same time the consultant works on the task-learning process: the analysis of market trends, the organization's past performance, and so on. The core of the integrative task is then

   (a) to identify such basic values as underlie both marketing (or whatever technical aspect is relevant) and interpersonal behaviour;
   (b) to discover aspects of the behavioural climate that might hamper an open and complete analysis of the task;
   (c) to discover the unmentionable task topics and bring them out into the open;
   (d) to facilitate communication in difficult technical fields where some of the participants might feel ignorant and therefore inferior;
   (e) to present new models for the analysis of old task problems so as to get the participants to focus on new dimensions of the problem, and
   (f) to help the participants to understand all kinds of interconnections between task and behaviour.

2. *The contract between the client and the consultant* needs to be continually revised. This is essential if the relationship between the two parties is to be adapted to the nature of the work in the different phases. People involved in a first phase which involves the definition of the problem and the choice of working methods and budget, may not be the same as those who work on the diagnosis. Again, different people may be concerned with decisions and implementation. Furthermore, the employee organizations are variously interested in influencing and participating in the different phases. It is therefore imperative that the contract – the economic contract as well as the social and psychological – be continually revised and the client remain observant of the contract's dynamic aspects.

3. *Shared responsibility in all phases* of the consultation process is necessary in order to break up the stereotypes of power and control. The all-important element here is valid feedback. The crucial process in all learning phases is the feedback process. Especially when working simultaneously with technical and behavioural problems it is of utmost importance that the feedback from the consultant to the client and vice versa be valid and testable. A prerequisite for the generation of data for valid and testable feedback is mutual trust. But how

does a consultant create trust? When a consultant assumes full responsibility for the technical solution, we could say that in a way he enjoys the client's complete trust. But this kind of trust has been placed beyond discussion and confrontation. It is a matter of either–or. The kind of trust we want to create is of a different nature. It must allow for confrontation, and it must leave the client with maximum freedom of choice at the different stages of the learning process. Ideally, the methods the consultant wants to use for collecting and feeding back information should be known, understood, and agreed upon before they are used. Best of all, the methods should be worked out together with the client. The ideal process would involve a dispersion of roles whereby client and consultant work together through a problem-solving sequence. Of fundamental importance is that both parties together decide at each step in the process how the roles should be divided and how valid feedback from consultant to client and vice versa should be arranged.

4. *The open character of the consultation process* is easy to talk about but often difficult to realize. If the organization's communication patterns and communication styles are efficient, a consultation process is likely to be handled in an open way. But if internal communications are one of the company's chief problems, the consultant will come up against the same difficulties as other members of the organization. If the climate in the organization is marked by mistrust, intergroup rivalry, string-pulling, and power struggles, then a consultant will find it very difficult to avoid being drawn into the game. For one thing, he is not sufficiently familiar with the internal game to defend himself, and for another he is not present in the client organization every day and cannot therefore control how, by whom, and for what purpose he is being used. Nor can he check what other people are saying about him.

In brief, it is important that the client understands the importance of an open approach to the consultation process. In an integrated development strategy process this awareness should develop in the course of the task, as participants learn from and about their own and other people's behaviour.

Results of an IDS Intervention

The open strategies that the consultant has used in collecting information and providing feedback, as well as the openness in his relations with the client, make him more accessible and available for confrontations. For instance, since he need not assume sole responsibility for the chosen diagnostic methods, it is easier for him to discuss constructively any objections to the methods or to their results. Because of the open strategies the client feels less defensive towards the consultant; and of course the strategies themselves represent an example of the kind of change the consultant is trying to promote.

In an IDS intervention various factors combine to enable the consultant–client relationship to develop synergistically, namely the open confrontations allowed for in the model, the kind of techniques and strategies that are used, and the human dynamics that are allowed for in the relationship itself. The special competences of the consultant and the client can be utilized to the full, since there are no obstacles in the shape of power games, defensive behaviour, or reciprocal manipulation.

The jointly agreed strategy for the consultancy project allows both client and consultant to experiment and try out ideas that may not appear likely at a first glance to provide solutions to the company's problems. It becomes possible to take risks, both in the relationship itself and in the problem for which solutions are being tested. The norms obtaining in the consultant–client relationship allow for greater openness and less fear of confrontation as well as encouraging a generally dynamic approach to the problems.

As a result of the open norms and the dynamic models used, the learning generated by the consultation is likely to be less specific to the single task and more easily generalized to other problems. The client learns how to make diagnoses, how to learn from experience, and how to set about initiating changes in his organization.

To learn how to learn from data and experience, to learn how to tackle new kinds of change, to learn how to test ideas against valid information instead of blindly falling in with certain axioms – all this constitutes genuine learning as opposed to the kind of thermostat or 'single loop' learning that we referred to before, whereby a set solution is automatically applied to a particular type of fault.

The open climate that evolves in the consultant–client relationship allows for mutual, testable, and flexible learning as opposed to the kind of private and untested learning that is common in many consultancy assignments. Since the open climate embraces the consultant, the client, and various other parties in the client organization, it can justifiably be called *organizational learning*.

Organizational learning can be productive, since it is based not on axioms but on actual observed data, and since it has evolved in an open process; the participants have learnt to analyse their problems together, to learn from their experiences, and to revise their learning continuously in mutual confrontations.

CHAPTER 5

The IDS Model

Two Main Ingredients of an IDS

Organizations exist in a continuous state of change, even when it seems to their members that everything is the same as it always has been. The shifts in values and priorities, in technology, and the distribution of power are often unnoticeable as they occur, so that only a long time afterwards can people see that a change has taken place. One of the things that can prevent people from realizing exactly what is going on is the discrepancy between the espoused organizational norms and the norms that are actually in use: sometimes there are spectacular changes in the espoused norms and none at all in the norms applied, and at other times it is the other way round.

Something else that may prevent people from seeing change, is that change or anything related to change may be an unmentionable topic. Thus if we want to make an adequate assessment of what an organization is and what it is not, the forces that prevent people from seeing what is happening must first be overcome. And this will only be possible if people can learn. Learning is therefore one main ingredient in an IDS intervention process.

Another important assumption underlying the IDS approach is that in the real world there are no boundaries between technical and social problems. People are 'behaving' at all stages in a 'technical' problem-solving process; they apply both their reason and their emotions to what is often thought of as a purely rational decision process. The problem-solvers themselves will probably not be aware of two 'processes'; they are simply doing the natural thing, namely taking action and making decisions which are the results of rational problem-solving and of social or interpersonal processes, without reflecting on the interconnectedness of the two. However, a consultant needs the concept of the dual process, so that he can relate what he does to the actions of other interventionists and researchers who are working on one of the processes only; he also needs it because it helps him and the client system to choose the appropriate techniques from those that are available at the different stages in the learning processes. Integration between task and behaviour is therefore the second major ingredient of an IDS.

Thus the IDS has two basic ingredients:

1. a learning approach to change;
2. a simultaneous focusing on task (marketing, production, etc.) and behaviour (individual, group, and organization).

A Learning Approach

The norms and control systems prevailing in an organization are mainly produced by the people working in the organization. These norms and systems will thus stem from the theories of action of the organization members.

If a far-reaching and durable change is to be effected in an organization, the theories that govern present behaviour will have to be altered. But the same people who have recognized that present norms or control systems, or their own ways of coping with things, are not proving effective in attaining the desired objectives, may be incapable of finding any new norms or control systems or personal action theories that would be better. Or, if they are capable of inventing new theories, they may lack the skills necessary for implementing them.

An effective organization must constantly test and revise its strategies in the various domains of marketing, finance, etc. This process can be illustrated by the strategy cycle already discussed in Chapter 2.

We thus have two similar learning cycles, one focused on business strategy and other organizational task issues, and the other on norms, control systems, and other organizational–behavioural issues (Figure 5.1).

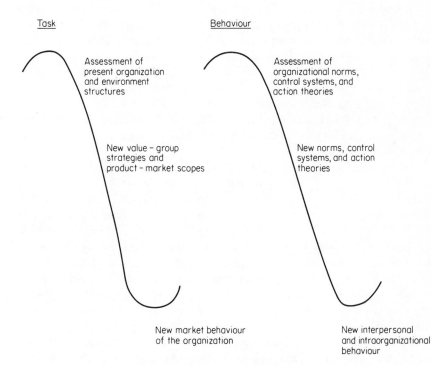

Figure 5.1. The IDS learning cycles

Integration of Task and Behaviour

Splitting the problem into two processes

The learning cycles serve mainly as an educational tool; in reality the dividing line is an artificial one. But the fact remains that in real life people do frequently think in such categories, although it is difficult to say whether this is due to formal training or to the habit of concealing so much of their personalities when acting in organizational contexts that 'interpersonal behaviour' comes to be regarded as a thing apart from problem-solving. (In our own work we have found that people become more upset and bothered at the thought of integrating the two processes than at being asked to accept an ad hoc dividing line between them.)

There are, however, other justifications for using the notion of two learning cycles, and these can now be explained in more detail.

First, the aim of an IDS is to improve task performance, not simply to make people feel happier or better pleased with one another; in fact, at least at the beginning of a process, the level of frustration and conflict may rise rather than fall. To make it possible to check periodically that events are moving in the right direction, some critical steps that lend themselves to evaluation must be incorporated into the learning cycle. Criteria of efficiency will be needed for this purpose, and these may conflict with such (overall) efficiency criteria as might be set up for the behavioural process if it were being viewed as the sole and most important process (as it is in T-groups or other kinds of sensitivity-group training).

Second, different techniques are available for getting the best out of the various learning steps in the task process. Choosing between the alternatives and the related actions is a difficult task for the interventionist – particularly because such things must be judged from the point of view of *both* the processes. Thus, thinking in terms of two learning cycles should make it easier to judge the alternatives and to choose between them.

Thinking and working in terms of two learning cycles thus enables the interventionist to design the appropriate action and judge its effectiveness at different stages in the processes. But – and this is a third justification for the two-pronged approach – it also more or less compels the interventionist (and the group) to face up to the problem of integrating knowledge from one learning cycle into the other. Suppose, for example, that a client has been closely scrutinizing some important behavioural norm prevailing in the group, a norm which in fact could also be fruitfully used in tackling some part of the task problem: how can the consultant make the client 'see' this? What activities will be the effective integrative ones? The consultant has to discover and demonstrate these so that the client becomes able to transfer his new knowledge to the task process.

Particularly in the early stages of the processes it is part of the interventionist's task to 'time' this sort of feedback in such a way that it will be as effective – and as little time-consuming – as possible. His own ideas about how much and how well people are learning will be based on his analytical observations of the two processes.

We know that when a group embarks on a difficult and complex task something will happen between the group members during the subsequent process. But should we regard these intragroup developments as being as important as the explicit task? Or is the prime function of IDS simply to provide a means of helping the interventionist?

To this last question we would like to answer both yes and no. Yes, because we have found in practice that the IDS approach does help the consultant to help the organization to move in new and difficult directions. No, because the underlying purpose of the IDS is of course to help the client to learn. People who have participated in an IDS process will have learnt a great deal about human dynamics in general and about their own behaviour in particular; on future occasions they should be more prepared to plan for their own learning and will consequently be capable of more effective problem-solving.

Integrating the learning cycles

The principles involved in integrating the two learning cycles are best explained by reference to empirical data. This will be presented in the studies described in Chapters 6 and 7. In the meantime we can outline the principles in theoretical terms, using the model of the two learning processes and adding a further process. This is the integration process whose purpose is to take appropriate action with regard to feedback. Thus the integration process does not consist of the client's learning; it consists of the interventionist's actions. Figure 5.2 gives an overall view of the integration process.

When moving from 'assessment' to 'invention' a person or a group will have:

1. used *data*;
2. interpreted the data in a *model*; and
3. drawn some *conclusions* from this.

The aim of the integration process is the transfer of some or all of these (i.e. data, models, or results) from one process to the other.

In other words the integration process can transfer either the *model* or the *data* or the *results*, or all three, from 'task assessment' to 'behavioural assessment' or vice versa. Let us give an example.

Suppose that a top executive group is about to review its business strategy, something that it does regularly. The sessions are not necessarily called into being as a result of any drastic external or internal changes; they are little more than a way of checking where the company stands and of increasing its preparedness for any major political, financial, or market changes in the future.

On one occasion there has been some important political change in the country; elections are to be held within a year and according to the opinion polls the

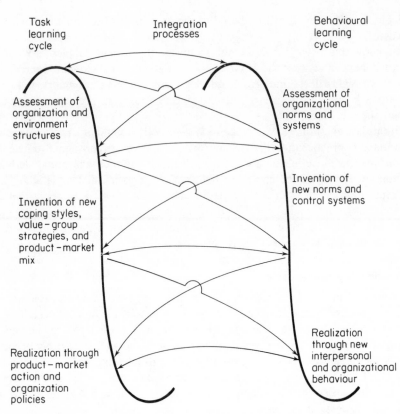

Task
learning
cycle

Integration
processes

Behavioural
learning
cycle

Assessment of
organization and
environment
structures

Assessment of
organizational
norms and
systems

Invention of new
coping styles,
value – group
strategies, and
product – market
mix

Invention of
new norms and
control systems

Realization through
product – market
action and
organization
policies

Realization
through new
interpersonal
and organizational
behaviour

Figure 5.2. The integration processes at different stages in IDS

largest opposition party is well to the fore. So there is a good chance of a new government taking over. The opposition's programme includes a new tax on production factors such as electronic computers which, if it were to be implemented, would greatly affect the cost situation of our organization. The relative cost of machinery and robots would increase and the automatization programme agreed upon two years ago would be less profitable than the original analysis predicted.

One member of the top executive group is suspected by the others of being a member of the opposition party. They have not openly taken the matter up with him, but they assume that he would probably do anything to be loyal to his political beliefs. Thus if it comes to reconsidering and possibly altering the programme previously agreed upon, they do not believe he will think of the company's best; they think he would rather see them stick to the earlier decision and pay bigger taxes. They also feel chary of discussing this openly in the group; when the first session is due, nobody raises the important 'political' issues although everyone knows that if they agree on the likelihood of a new tax policy they might also want to revise their decisions on future business strategy, at least as far as the introduction of the new computers is concerned.

When asked why they are reluctant to talk about future political developments and the possible effects that the election may have on their company, they talk convincingly about 'not interfering with people's political opinions', 'business and politics shouldn't be mixed' and so on. But when it is pointed out to them by the consultants that by 'protecting' member A's political integrity and privacy they are violating this very norm, they say they are defending people's freedom to believe whatever they want. (If people are trusted with their own opinions, why not talk openly about them?) In this case the protective attitude is inhibiting any deeper analysis of the possible automation programme and, consequently of personnel policy and other related problems. The kind of feedback needed here would help the group to see that they are in fact protecting their colleague in order to keep things comfortable for themselves, although they have convinced themselves they are doing it in his best interests. The feedback would also help them to see that they cannot make a serious strategic diagnosis of the environment of their company if they cannot openly discuss 'political matters'.

We have in fact been describing a real case in which feedback of the kind suggested was supplied. Eventually the group learned to discuss and analyse several alternative political scenarios, and they decided to present some alternative 'degrees of automation' to the shareholders and to let them partake of the responsibility for the future of the company.

In this example the model of analysis (the norms) and the results (negative behaviour) had been transmitted from the behavioural process to the task process. A similar analysis can be applied to the case of, for instance, conservative task behaviour. Suppose that a company is unwilling to take risks when it comes to new products or markets; we can then ask ourselves whether similar conservatism and low risk-taking is evident in interpersonal behaviour in the company as well, and if so whether the same norm is perhaps governing both the product and market behaviour *and* interpersonal behaviour. If such norms are discovered, the consultant and the client may then be able to create new and more productive norms, and to discuss together how these could be applied in both the interpersonal and the technical domains.

It should be noted, though, that all three ingredients (model, data, and results) do not necessarily have to be transferred from one process to another. The consultant may choose to pick some particular set of data, a particular model, or some specific results for the integration. And integration can be effected entirely by the interventionist or as a result of the client's direct experience. If the consultant does most of the integration work on his own and exposes the client only to a small part of it, we can speak of *bypass integration*. If the consultant invites the client to participate in the integration work, we can speak of *experiential integration*. Let us now explore these two types of integration in more detail.

A Bypass Integration Strategy

Bypass integration is based on the hypothesis that the interventionist assumes responsibility for the development of the processes. This means that he first makes a diagnosis and then unilaterally designs such action as he believes will overcome any obstacles that appear likely to hamper the learning processes.

He may have discovered, for example, that some organizational norm stops people talking about failed products. At the same time he probably feels that an open discussion and analysis of past failures is necessary if new strategies are to be designed for launching new products effectively. Thus he has to find ways of making it possible to discuss failure. The interventionist is faced with the problem illustrated in Figure 5.3.

In a bypass integration process the interventionist tries to find *the quickest way of making it possible to discuss this particular type of failure, in order to solve this particular task problem.* In other words he does not look for ways of changing the organizational norm that makes failure a taboo subject; he simply seeks a way of overcoming the power of the norm on this particular occasion. He may do this by *modelling his own behaviour* in such a way that *failure no longer seems taboo in the relevant content.* Or he may try to reinvoke some failures committed in the past, in which other people were involved, to show that failure is something which can and does happen elsewhere in the organization. Or he may refer to case studies of failure in other organizations, to show that failure can and does happen elsewhere in the industry. And there are certainly many other ways of breaking the taboos. The aim of all these attempts, however, is to reduce the threat associated with *violating a particular norm on a particular occasion* (Figure 5.4).

There are several reasons why a bypass integration strategy may be appropriate. First, it helps to save time during the discovery phase. Second, it is useful as a way of preparing the client, if the interventionist finds such preparation

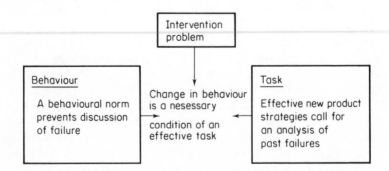

Figure 5.3. An intervention problem

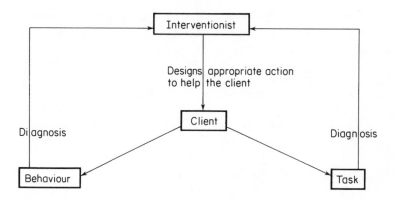

Figure 5.4. A model of bypass integration

to be necessary. Third, the contract between the interventionist and the client may not permit the interventionist to go beyond certain specified questions. Last, it may be motivated by the hierarchic level of the client, or his power to question norms of the kind that the interventionist is subjecting to review.

Any of these reasons may legitimately motivate the use of a bypass integration strategy. On the other hand it should be remembered that this strategy can never provide the client with as much learning and insight as the kind of experiential integration strategy that will be described below. Experiential learning is also necessary for tackling problems that seriously question current strategies or policies.

An Experiential Integration Strategy

When the client takes an active part in the integration process we can speak of experiential integration. The interventionist is still responsible for designing the integrative activities but he invites the client to join him in his learning cycles. This means that the interventionist strives to achieve a joint diagnosis, and he shares his experiences with the client along the way. The client on his part is prepared to accept feedback regarding both task and behaviour which may sometimes be difficult to stomach, and he assumes responsibility for handling this feedback and learning from it.

If a specific organizational norm is incompatible with effective action, the interventionist who has decided on an experiential strategy is responsible for feeding back this information to the client. As the information is threatening, it may be difficult to pass it on, and because it is threatening the client may not enjoy receiving it. It should also be remembered that what the interventionist is feeding back is only a hypothesis, often bearing little resemblance to the

54

'conventional wisdom' of the organization. He may not even be certain that he is right – whether he has really seen what he thinks he has seen, and whether what he has seen means what it seems to mean.

Thus there are many difficulties to be overcome in applying an experiential integration process. Let us return to the example we have already mentioned. *Failure is a taboo subject, but some particular failure has got to be discussed in order to solve a task problem.* The interventionist then has to bring this problem out into the open together with the client, and in doing so he has to try to find answers to questions such as the following:

1. Failure seems to be a forbidden topic – why?
2. What is it about failure that makes this client unable to discuss it?
3. How and why has failure become a forbidden topic?
4. Can the client recall any particular failure he has experienced? If so, can the client be specific and detailed about the nature of the failure?
5. If the client admits that the failure had to be covered up, why was this so?
6. What is the cover-up process doing to the client?

The interventionist faces the same basic questions as in the previous example, namely: 'How can we get things done despite the dysfunctional behavioural processes?' 'How do I tell the clients that they must tackle a problem that violates a basic norm of their organization?' But in an experiential situation he will add the important questions: 'How do I prove to myself and to them that my observations

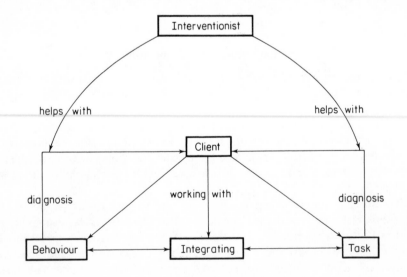

Figure 5.5. A model of experiential integration

are correct?' 'What data, what collecting process, and what models will support my observations?'

Conceptually the experiential integration strategy differs from the bypass strategy in that the interventionist's role is to help the client to embark on an assessment–invention–realization cycle without being secretive.

A Comparison Between the Bypass and the Experiential IDS

The main feature of experiential integration is that it makes it possible for the client to assess, invent, and realize in both the behavioural and the task cycles. Thus the experiential strategy encourages more extensive and more comprehensive learning, whereas bypass integration restricts itself mainly to getting things done, and any learning that occurs is of secondary importance. But it is not at all easy to control an experiential integration strategy. In the cases described in Chapters 6 and 7 we will illustrate several examples of bypass and experiential integration. It should be noted, however, that the two types of IDS are not mutually exclusive and/or incompatible with one another. On the contrary, the interventionist will probably find himself compelled in the course of a change process to employ a mixture of bypassing and experiential activities.

Bypassing and experiential activities can be regarded as extremes on a continuum of honesty or openness. The more unclassified the information which the interventionist passes on to the client, the deeper and more sincere will be the dialogue between them. But such an approach also tends to increase the time required for the process, and thus of course also its cost. An experienced interventionist knows when he can use bypassing without too much damage to the quality of the client's learning process. Not enough empirically based research has yet been reported to justify any comparison of the relative success and effectiveness of the different intervention styles. But the following are some very general ideas about the variables that probably affect the essentially intuitive choice made by the consultant:

1. At what stage in the intervention process are we?
   In our opinion it is almost impossible to start an intervention process with experiential activities. The client and the consultant have to get to know one another before the basic trust necessary to this kind of collaboration can be established.
2. In what phase of the learning cycle are we?
   If the client's problem concerns the sort of task of which the consultant has considerable experience, and if the consultant has reason to believe that analysing the problem in cases of this sort normally takes a very long time, he will probably feel inclined to get the process started by using bypass methods in the discovery phase, and then gradually to introduce more experiential activities when it comes to invention and implementation of new solutions.

3. What resources are available?

More resources are probably needed for an experiential intervention. When you lack time, for example, it is easier to give an order than to embark on a persuasive dialogue. We would even suggest that one of the consultant's responsibilities is to check on the available resources before launching an experiential learning process. If time or other resources are short, it may sometimes be a good idea to postpone experiential activities, particularly if the consultant, with future activities in mind, takes the trouble to gather and store information (e.g. tapes of meetings) for use in a later phase.

PART II

Cases

Introduction to the Cases

The cases presented in Chapters 6 and 7 are seen from the consultant's point of view. They are described in such a way as to illustrate the two kinds of IDS discussed above in Chapter 5. They are also designed to illustrate the various aspects of strategy, organizational learning, and intervention that were discussed in the earlier chapters of Part I.

However, it should be noted that the theory presented in Part I also embodies what we ourselves learnt from working with IDS in the two development processes described in Part II. Thus the cases do not always reflect all the features of the theory, which is sometimes more far-reaching and systematized than the practical consultations ever were.

All case descriptions involve the writer in a dilemma; truth has to be balanced against the protection of the people and the organizations concerned. We have taken most of the material presented below from two specific interventions in two organizations. For the sake of preserving their anonymity we refer to the organizations as Alpha and Beta. We have also altered some aspects both of the organizations themselves and of the people involved. Further, we have added certain intervention actions and organizational processes from other cases in order to make the descriptions more fruitful and to clarify other sides of the intervention process.

In this way we hope that we have produced descriptions which meet two demands:

1. that they cannot be related direct to any specific organizations or people; and
2. that they should provide useful and illustrative material for the reader seeking a fuller understanding of IDS.

CHAPTER 6

A Bypass IDS – The Alpha Case

Synopsis

In this chapter we shall describe an intervention in a strategy formulation process. The client organization operates in the insurance industry and our purpose has been to describe the processes that evolved in a key group engaged in the re-formulation of the company's business strategy in response to identified and expected environmental changes. It will be shown how an integrated development strategy (IDS) and the related intervention actions during the learning phases of assessment, invention, and realization, helped the organization to develop more effective ways of dealing with its environment.

The chapter is written in the first person singular, since one of the present authors acted as consultant to the company concerned and was in direct contact with the client. The second author acted as a shadow consultant.

Background to the Assignment and Description of the Organization

In the early spring of 1972 I was contacted by a representative of a group of insurance companies which I shall refer to below as 'Alpha'. The company's representative introduced himself as the marketing director of the organization, and he asked to see me to discuss an urgent problem connected with market planning. I agreed to meet him at his office a few days later.

At this first meeting the marketing director gave me a general description of Alpha. The organization consisted of 66 autonomous consumer-owned insurance companies which collaborated in different ways through a common association. The joint association did not itself undertake any operations; operational responsibility was vested instead in an organization owned by the joint association, and referred to below as the *central organization*.

The highest decision-making body in the joint association was an assembly consisting of representatives from all the autonomous companies, which normally met once a year. The regular decision unit of the association was its board of directors. The board included an executive committee, which in fact was identical with the board of directors of the central organization. The ownership structure of Alpha is illustrated in Figure 6.1.

The 66 insurance companies were all autonomous, but they were guided to a

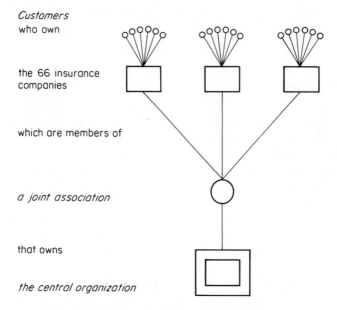

Figure 6.1. The ownership structure of Alpha

great extent on questions of policy by recommendations from the board of directors and the executive committee of the joint association. These recommendations were normally prepared by groups consisting of members of some of the autonomous companies plus one or two members (specialists) of the central organization. Among these groups were the *marketing group* (the subject of this study) which had been created primarily to deal with questions of long-range strategic interest, and the *organization group*, created to deal with long-range structural questions in the organization. The questions handled by these groups were generally prepared by employees of the central organization for further discussion in the group concerned. Finally a formal recommendation based on the decisions of the group was passed on to the companies by the board of directors of the association. The autonomous companies complied with the recommendations in varying degrees and with varying modifications, depending on the market situation and the organizational characteristics and financial conditions of the company concerned.

The competitive structure of the Swedish insurance industry at the beginning of the 1970s can be described as strongly oligopolistic. The various companies carried rather similar products, they specialized on different market segments, the competition between them was characterized by conjectural behaviour such as price leadership and product imitation; furthermore, in certain segments both price and product competition could become extremely keen, while in others a single company dominated and competition was practically non-existent except as a constant threat. There was also evident awareness of the complex inter-dependence between insurance companies and other large organizational units in various sectors of society.

The marketing group

Technical questions of insurance and administrative processes had traditionally dominated the collaboration between the companies in Alpha. But as new product lines were adopted in the late 1960s and new markets conquered in the early 1970s, marketing and relations with the environment in general began to occupy an increasingly prominent position. The general trend towards concentration in the insurance industry reinforced this development. A marketing group was formed in 1968 to analyse Alpha's market relations and to develop a market planning system. It was realized that before any such system could be launched, however, the problem of organizational goals and competitive profile would first have to be carefully gone into. The question of formulating a strategy was thus postponed.

The marketing group had five members. Group member A had previously been marketing director in the central organization; he became president of one of the independent companies in 1971. Because of his present and earlier position, he was regarded by several other company executives as a person of considerable influence.

Group member B was also president of one of the member companies. He had been chosen primarily because he was on the executive committee of the joint association.

Group member C was president of one of the biggest companies in the organization. On several occasions this company had taken action independently of the others, and C played a leading role among the more 'independent-minded' company presidents.

Member D was chairman of the group. He had been chosen, as member A put it, 'because of his high status and the good reputation he enjoyed in the organiza-tion'. He held a doctor's degree (members A and B had first degrees in the same subject). He had been a researcher in the field of agriculture before becoming an executive in the insurance business.

Group member E had been marketing director of the central organization since the beginning of 1972. His membership and his position as secretary of the group was motivated by his function in the organization.

All this was told me by the marketing director (E). I then asked for more details about the project. E continued:

> 'The marketing group was formed a couple of years ago to analyse the market situation of the organization and to develop a market-planning system. I didn't belong to the group then. It was A, who is now presi-dent of company A, who at that time was director of marketing and

secretary of the marketing group. At that time the group considered that its first task was to create and promote the idea of a common name and a common symbol for all member companies. Later, when they started seriously on the market-planning project, they felt that problems of organizational goals should be analysed first, and to that end another group was formed. This latter group had chosen to write a goal statement for a "model company" – that is, a non-existent company with features typical of a majority of the member companies. By and by the group started to work on the market-planning project, with A acting as secretary of the group.

But A soon became president of company A, and the group chose a new secretary, Z. Z tried all sorts of approaches; he attended executive courses in marketing and planning and studied some of the generally accepted books in this field. But still the group did not seem to get anywhere. As the result of a reorganization, Z moved to another function in the central organization. I [it is still E speaking] was eventually appointed director of marketing, and thereby automatically secretary of the marketing group.'

In our further discussions E was eager to emphasize the complexity of the problems, and to stress his own inability to find a systematic approach to the problem because of his limited theoretical background. He kept saying that what both he and the group now needed was some kind of systematic approach – preferably a checklist or a manual for market planning. Finally we agreed that I should think things over and try to come up with a suitably systematic approach.

My conclusions from the first meeting with the client

According to E the group's failure to develop a market plan depended on its inability to find a systematic approach to the problem, and this in turn depended on insufficient knowledge of planning theory and models. But the group had already been working for a considerable period, between one and two years, on the market-planning project; also, before E joined them, two previous secretaries had spent a good deal of time trying to find an appropriate approach to the task. Z had apparently also made himself familiar with the theories presented in the current literature of the subject.

Thus I concluded from what E told me that lack of knowledge of formal planning models could not be the only thing that had prevented the group from fulfilling its task.

I realized, of course, that there could be many reasons for the failure. After my first meeting with E, I felt inclined to add the following factors to those which he had emphasized. First, it seemed to me that on the whole the company presidents were anxious to remain as independent as possible of the central organization. This meant that several members of the group – which had been composed to reflect as many key groups as possible – may have been primarily interested in seeing that no common strategy was ever actually formulated. Second, E referred repeatedly to the fact that he had no university degree and no theoretical qualifications of any other kind, whereas in describing the other group members he was careful to mention their formal academic merits. I concluded from this that his non-academic status made him feel inferior to the other group members, and that perhaps he was generally unsure of himself. Was E looking to me to provide him with the expert authority he believed was necessary to persuade the other group members of his own views?

Finally, I concluded from what E told me about two previous secretaries (of whom at least one had acquainted himself with much of the relevant literature on planning and marketing), that something more than mere lack of knowledge must be hampering efficiency.

Assessment

Planned intervention for the first group meeting

For the first meeting with the group my main intervention goals were to get the members of the group to put into words what they knew and believed about the organization and its major competitive advantages and disadvantages. I also wanted to get everyone to feel free and relaxed, so that we could work creatively together. I hoped, too, to establish an easy and informal relationship between myself and the other group members. Finally, I wanted us all to share responsibility for the outcome of the meeting; in this way, I reasoned, the company presidents would feel committed to the task and I would not have to speculate anxiously about their possibly unrealistic expectations regarding my own contribution.

Eventually I chose the following actions to attain my goals.

1. One week before the meeting a questionnaire was sent to all group members. My idea was to encourage them to think in dimensions relevant to an evaluation of the organization and its position on the market, and to help them individually to make up their minds on various points and to work out why they thought as they did. I then hoped to get them all to motivate their standpoints at the group sessions and to thrash out any conflicting opinions among themselves. The questionnaire had been constructed in such a way that each respondent could evaluate the competitive standing of the organization from $+10$ (major competitive advantage) to -10 (major competitive disadvantage). At the group session all members would report their scores and their main reasons for having chosen a particular standpoint.

   Evaluations were requested separately, in 18 dimensions, for every product in the different market segments. The disposition of the questionnaire can be seen in Figure 6.2. (The segments corresponded to those used in the marketing

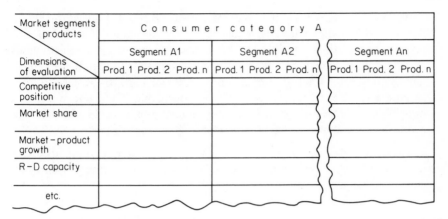

Market segments / products — Dimensions of evaluation	Consumer category A								
	Segment A1			Segment A2			Segment An		
	Prod. 1	Prod. 2	Prod. n	Prod. 1	Prod. 2	Prod. n	Prod. 1	Prod. 2	Prod. n
Competitive position									
Market share									
Market – product growth									
R – D capacity									
etc.									

Figure 6.2. The design of the questionnaire

department of the central organization, with reference to the current marketing activities which they sponsored.)

Altogether the group was to produce over one thousand scores. I hoped in this way to get a comprehensive survey of the members' ideas about the strengths and the weaknesses of their organization. In discussing each item, members were also asked to assess the importance of the relevant dimensions – segment/product – and to say why they thought it was important (they were to compare with possible competitor's items, to consider the threats or opportunities associated with the particular item, to try to assess the time span and probable evolution of the opportunities or threats, and so on). I thus hoped to ensure that all relevant aspects would be considered, but that only those dimensions that were crucial to future success would be analysed in detail.

2. In addition to this questionnaire and the unstructured discussion that I hoped would arise from it, I had prepared certain questions about the feelings, hopes, and fears of the group members on certain specific issues. I was prepared to ask questions such as: 'You have put a +5 for this item – can you tell us something about the way you reached this score?' or, 'Member A has a negative evaluation here – what is your reaction to this?' These questions were intended to give group members an opportunity to motivate their evaluations and to reflect, for instance, on any possible uncertainties or risks associated with them. The questions were also intended to encourage open and trusting behaviour, as well – I hoped – as giving the participants a sense of psychological security.

3. My third set of planned actions consisted of modelling my own behaviour in such a way that the members of the group would feel free to make suggestions, to ask questions even if they felt they 'ought' to know the answers, and to say

what they felt even if it did not seem immediately relevant. I hoped to achieve this by asking apparently naive questions, by suggesting far-fetched and possibly unrealistic solutions to problems, and by referring disrespectfully to ideas and convictions that I believed to be firmly established in the organization. By doing this I hoped to break down inhibitions and to encourage others to be a little less respectful as well. I reasoned that if a group norm was 'prohibiting' people from saying anything stupid, no one would ever dare risk expressing an unconventional or 'new' idea.

As we were to dine out together in the course of the two-day group session, I knew I would have an opportunity to build up a more personal relationship with the individual members of the group.

I met member E several times while I was preparing the questionnaire and the other questions; I wanted to get as much information from him as possible about the organization and the group before our first meeting, and I even discussed with him some of the actions I had planned.

The first group meeting

The first group meeting took place in June 1972 at the central organization. Present were the four company presidents (A, B, C, and D), the director of marketing (E), and myself. The meeting lasted for two days; it included lunch both days and dinner at a restaurant on the first evening.

After member E had introduced me to the rest of the group, and the individual members to me, I told them my reasons for sending out the questionnaire and explained how I thought we should use it. I then added that I had prepared some additional questions to help me to cover certain aspects of the organization not included in the questionnaire. Finally, I expressed the hope that we would be able to communicate in a free and relaxed way.

Member A then complained quite spontaneously about the amount of work involved in filling in the questionnaire, and he was supported by the other three company presidents. I answered jokingly, probably because I felt embarrassed by A's critical remarks; I was only too aware of the tremendous number of items I had confronted them with. However, I got some support from member E who argued that this was probably the best way of tackling the problem. D smoothed over the slight controversy by stating firmly that he believed in this approach, and he received unanimous support from the others.

After this short argument the chairman suggested that we should begin to discuss the items on the questionnaire one by one. Normally I introduced the consumer category, while E and A, who had both been involved in the analysis on which the segmentation criteria were based, gave a brief survey of the principles which had been applied there. There was very little discussion about the relevance of the segments, but everyone tacitly agreed with everything that was said. I then introduced the first dimension – competitive position – and asked one of the presidents for his evaluations. He told us the scores he had given and the main reasons for his choice. I asked the other group members if their evaluations were any different, but their accounts were almost identical to the first speaker's. So it continued item by item. Eventually I tried to ask rather provocative questions, such as:

> 'But B, how can you put +5 here? I can understand C doing so because of the circumstances in his company, but it's surely different for you?'
> B: 'All right, there may be some differences in our circumstances, but I don't think they should be exaggerated – we shouldn't forget the similarities! There may also be some differences between the way we have defined +5 in this particular instance . . . .'

I sensed a strong norm in the group according to which members should try to conform and not to question the judgements of their peers. However, I did not feel that I could produce any remedy for this, other than the intervention actions described above.

The first day of the first meeting proceeded slowly. One market segment after another was discussed, the pattern of communication remaining much the same throughout the day. I did not find many opportunities for provoking group members to make any firm stands; nor did I have much occasion to be frank, open, or bold, in a way that would inspire the others to openness and frankness. On the contrary, I felt during the afternoon of the first day that I was largely conforming to what was apparently a group norm of conservatism and politeness.

At dinner on the first day, member A criticized me for not pushing the group harder. I did not feel too embarrassed or surprised by the remark, as I interpreted his statement as a sign of frustration similar to my own over everybody's smooth and conservative behaviour. So I told A that I was not too pleased either, and that we should all try to be more free and open and not so careful and conservative in our evaluations. A agreed with me.

During dinner that first evening the group members developed a freer style of communication, but they remained as conservative and closed about the task as they had been during the day. No-one brought up any subject that embarrassed anybody else, and all discussion remained on a very social and general level.

The second day proceeded in the same way, except that all the members appeared a little more relaxed. As I found the atmosphere lighter and less tense, I felt more inspired to live up to my ideals of being open and venturesome. I suggested 'theoretical' ideas, drew parallels with other firms and industries – particularly with firms that had failed because of organizational and market myopia.

I even told the story of the boiled frog:

> 'You know what happens if you put a frog in a pan, put the pan on the stove, and slowly raise the heat? Well, as you know, the frog can jump

out of the pan whenever it likes, but when you put the heat on the frog grows lazier and lazier in the warm water. It's so nice and comfortable that the frog doesn't notice the danger. The warmer it gets, the lazier he becomes. Eventually the frog realizes it's too hot, but by that time he's too lazy and weak to jump – and so the poor thing boils to death . . . .'

And I asked if they could see any resemblance between this story and the cases of market myopia that I had also told them about. All sorts of suggestions and questions came up: 'Who was the frog? How about company X? Wasn't the whole insurance industry like the frog in the pan?' And so on.

The members of the group reacted positively to this freer and more relaxed approach. I made better eye contact with them; I also noticed that they became more expressive, reacting with laughter, smiles, nods, and even objections.

By the end of the second day we had gone through the whole questionnaire. B and D remarked quite spontaneously that we seemed to have accomplished a great deal during the two days, that we had in fact made substantial progress. A and C agreed, but did not say anything else particularly positive. E agreed with everyone and looked pleased. I also expressed my satisfaction with the meeting and pointed out that the questionnaire had been useful after all, since it had brought all the evaluations together and given them a systematic shape. This, I said, had given us a platform for our subsequent analysis. We finally agreed that, with some assistance from myself, E should collate the evaluations agreed upon by the group and distribute a copy of them to the other members as soon as possible.

At the end of the meeting, however, I was left with another impression which I had not mentioned. I had seen group members exchanging ideas in a way that could, according to conventional criteria, be described as efficient. Over a period of two days they had discussed a pretty comprehensive set of evaluations and arrived at common conclusions with very little argument. They also claimed to be pleased and to feel that progress had been made. I doubted this, however; and I wondered whether they were simply pleased that the session was over. All in all I suspected that something must be wrong. So I decided to listen to the tapes of the meeting, to see whether there was anything in my behaviour or in theirs which could explain my suspicion.

Reflections on the efficiency of the first meeting

I started my analysis of the tapes by focusing on the group's communication pattern. I used the Bales technique (Bales and Strodtbeck, 1968) and my 'shadow consultant' made an independent coding. We came to very similar results, which were as follows: 90% of the oral communications consisted of my asking for information (Bales 7) or for an opinion (Bales 8), and of one group member giving information (Bales 6) or an opinion (Bales 5). The rest of the oral communications consisted of various sorts of tension release (Bales 2), and a few expressions of disagreement (Bales 10). Although this analysis reflected oral communication only, and the style of total communication including eye contacts, smiles, gestures, etc. did in fact improve considerably between the first and second days, there was nevertheless no doubt that the free and relaxed communication between group members and between the group and myself, which had been one of my principal goals for the meeting, had not occurred to the extent that I had hoped. The communication style had improved but not as much as I thought necessary to effective group problem-solving.

Another of my goals had been to get group members to say what they knew and felt about the organization and its relations with the environment; I also wanted to arouse a feeling of commitment to our joint task, so that responsibility for the outcome would not rest entirely on my shoulders. I had hoped that the questionnaire and my other interview questions, together with the way I modelled my own behaviour, would help me to achieve this goal. But besides revealing the stereotyped communication pattern described above, the tapes also showed that we were all agreeing with one another on practically every question that came up. Surely it was rather surprising that although the group members worked in different kinds of regions and belonged to separate companies each with special traditions, and probably special organizational characteristics, they nevertheless arrived at almost identical evaluations of the organization? When I tried to provoke a more open discussion by asking further questions, I noticed that as soon as one member explained why he had chosen a particular rating the others were quick to agree with him, anxious to show that they felt just the same and had followed just the same line of reasoning. Instead of openness, trust, and individualistic behaviour (all of which seemed to me desirable and even necessary to the efficiency of the group decision process), I found smooth conformist behaviour and conservative and tentative expressions of opinion. The integration of the members' information took place through me; almost all communication assumed the shape of my asking someone a question, which he then answered, often seeking – and immediately receiving – support from the others.

Some possible unintended consequences of my intervention actions

The first method (intervention action) that I employed was to distribute the questionnaire. I designed this myself (although member E helped a little). The questionnaire was an attempt on my part to make sense of my clients' world. This meant that I assumed the responsibility for the diagnosis, which in turn implied a violation of my own goal – namely, to share responsibility for the outcome with the others. Further, as a questionnaire imposes a very formal way of asking questions, it may actually have prevented the others from being informal, free, and relaxed, or from expressing themselves in a creative way. Thus to some extent my intervention strategy seems to have counteracted my own objectives. The formalized questions may have helped me to keep control of events, thus reducing my own anxiety; but they may also have reinforced the very processes I was hoping to be able to change.

In addition to the questionnaire, I had also prepared another battery of questions. Thus the group would see that I had come armed with reserves, which they may have interpreted as meaning that I had decided in advance on an alternative strategy in case the first one did not work. This confirmed my assumption of responsibility for the success or failure of the group – which may have been just what they wanted!

Another element in my theory of intervention consisted of keeping my plans secret from the others. Only thus could I use the modelling of my own behaviour as part of my method. Asking naive questions or behaving disrespectfully can only work if nobody knows what you are doing. If it works, it is of course meant to provoke the others to behave more openly; but by keeping my own strategy secret I may instead have been promoting secrecy in the others, both towards me and among themselves. The group members may all have had secret strategies in relation to me, perhaps reflecting a theory in use whereby people skilfully and purposefully manipulate one another, without anyone admitting it. Such a practice would also mean that if anyone became embarrassed, the others would rush to protect him – typical behaviour in an organization where people rarely confront one another.

The tapes also revealed several occasions on which I mistrusted the others. An example was my question to B quoted above: 'But B, how can you put +5 here? I can understand C doing so because of the circumstances in his company, but it's surely different for you?', which certainly meant that at that point I mistrusted B, and he may have understood this without saying so. But I never actually declared openly that I mistrusted anyone. In other words I was not even trying to act with genuine openness, in a way that might have helped to generate the kind of group dynamics I was striving for.

Thus my questionnaire, my own adoption of the group norms and my secretive intervention actions may all have served to reinforce the very behaviour that I was hoping to change.

Goals and actions planned for the second meeting

From the tapes of the first meeting I not only learnt something about the processes that had operated there, I was also able to identify certain structural properties of the group and of the organization as a whole which seemed to explain the limited success of the meeting. In the course of preparing for the second meeting, I talked individually to all the group members, and on a basis of these interviews and the tapes I formed certain hypotheses about the group and the organization to which its members belonged.

As regards the group I hypothesized that negative effects had stemmed from the equal distribution of (quite substantial) power, the low degree of interdependence, the high degree of potential intragroup competitiveness, and the low level of differentiation. In the case of the organization it seemed that the poor quality of the information systems and the highly decentralized structure of the organization were probably the main cause of the failure of the strategy formulation process. Starting from these hypotheses and adopting a bypass strategy, I planned my subsequent actions with a view to overcoming the effects of these factors on our present project.

First, I decided to open our next session by discussing what I regarded as likely to be low-threat topics. If my hypothesis about the existence of latent competition among the company presidents was correct, the discussion of some low-threat topic should give the group members a greater sense of psychological security. And this, I hoped, would increase their (and my) willingness to take risks and to become less conformist. If we became more venturesome, less conformist, and more individualistic, it should also become possible to proceed more efficiently. I chose 'the local nature of the organization' as a low-threat and highly communicable topic, and based my new questions on the feedback from the first meeting that had been distributed to all group members by E.

Second, I decided to analyse individual problems with the help of alternative models. My purpose here was to probe the tacit models on which some of the members' evaluations had been based, thereby gently beginning to question some of the established beliefs of the organization.

Third, I decided to ask follow-up questions: 'Now, how do you do that?' 'Who does this?' 'Can you give me a recent example of that?' and so on – likely to lead to quite concrete or factual discussion. I wanted to make group members produce specific evidence, and to start talking about their practical experiences with one another.

Fourth, I decided to try to shake the 'conservative' attitude towards investing personnel and other resources in projects of the present kind. I hoped to do this by briefly describing what some other (successful) organizations had done on the same front.

For geographical reasons, and because of the organizational arrangements, I had most frequent contact with member E in the course of my preparations. This, I felt, was a good thing, because E knew the organization through and through and could provide me with a lot of information, while I could contribute with the more general frame of reference. However, I was also aware of the risk of creating two subgroups, with E and myself constituting a kind of 'staff' or working group, and the others turning into a passive audience. I could not think of any specific way of counteracting this, but I thought that if I discussed the problem with the group, their very awareness of the risk might prevent its possible negative effects.

Finally, I decided to continue using a rather smooth and tentative intervention style (as opposed to a more aggressive style involving confrontations etc.), as I believed that both parties – the group and myself – needed a considerable measure of psychological security if we were to be able to go on with the project at all. This seemed to me to be of paramount importance in such a highly decentralized organization, in which the autonomy of the different parts had apparently almost entirely precluded any kind of confrontation. If we were to succeed in formulating a strategy, the group had to become, in itself, an interdependent system.

The first day of the second group meeting

For certain unforeseen reasons group member E was unable to attend on the first day of the meeting. I saw this as an opportunity to try to reduce the risk of a line–staff conflict, and to assuage any potential rivalry between the presidents. In this way I also hoped to create a less conformist, more open-minded atmosphere, so that questions and answers could be equally distributed among group members and conflicting ideas could be brought out into the open.

The first subject I introduced was the possible competitive advantage to be gained from the decentralized organizational structure. The issue was of course relevant, as it was one of many factors on which the strategy was to be based, but my main reason for choosing this particular subject was another: I felt that all the presidents would be able to discuss it, without any one of them feeling less successful or less well-informed than the others.

The following conversation can illustrate the type of questions and answers triggered off by the written feedback everyone had received from E. (When this conversation took place, the general greetings and social chit-chat were over and the session proper was beginning.)

Interventionist: In the material you have received, which is based on our discussions last time, the 'local' nature of the companies is claimed as an advantage. If it is in fact an advantage, how do you exploit it, D?

D: It's really rather difficult to explain the advantages of being local in concrete terms.

Interventionist: A, can you tell me what local contacts you have, compared with your competitors?

A: There are several dimensions. We have already emphasized the board of directors, the employers and our home-based spare-time employees, and perhaps we should also discuss the position of the president . . . (A goes on to give details of what he considers to be the advantages of possessing local status.)

D: (Ṭaking up spontaneously one of A's ideas.) The advantages are more marked in the country, no doubt about that, and (goes on to say why) . . . .

Interventionist: But I thought competitor X had the same organizational set-up in this respect. So surely they must enjoy the same advantage?

A: Not in the same way. They have a similar technical structure but they are connected with different organizations. (A continues to expatiate on the differences between our organization and competitor X in this respect.)

C: (Interrupts spontaneously.) I would just like to add one point we often say that we 'belong', etc. (C elaborates something that A had just said.)

The sort of communication exemplified here continued to develop, and after a while the presidents started to comment and object, and to add fresh information or comments in direct connection with one another's questions. And, although they did not put questions directly to one another, the interaction between them was becoming freer and more relaxed. Throughout that day the tendency towards a free-and-easy pattern of communication grew more marked, and I even found the opportunity to take up some of the questions which I had designed specifically to provoke comparisons between two companies or two presidents in non-sensitive dimensions.

Analysis of the first day of the second meeting

After the first day I checked my tape-recordings against a Bales analysis (Figure 6.3) to see whether it bore out my impression that a freer and more open pattern

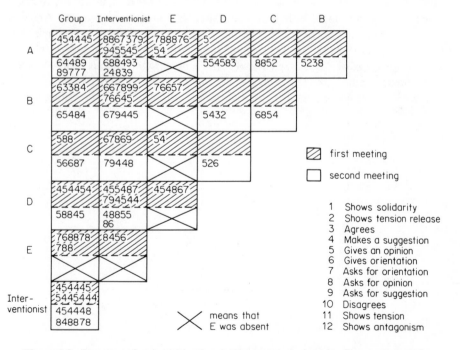

Figure 6.3. Patterns of communication in the group during the first and second meetings

of communication had begun to emerge. Figure 6.3 shows how the pattern changed between the first and second meetings. My own impression had been that the communication style of the group had improved, and the Bales analysis confirmed this. (The figure shows the results of the coding of tapes from the second hour of the first day of the two meetings.)

Although the Bales analysis supported my impression that group dynamics had improved (i.e. that the group was operating more efficiently), it was not certain that this was the result of my intervention. It might simply have been that as we began to get used to one another, or as the others began to feel safe with me (or even that they could control me), group members naturally became more relaxed. But whatever the cause of the improvement, it could be expected to have a positive effect on performance. It should also be remembered that the group had already been working for almost two years on the project, and this was the first major breakthrough in group behaviour.

Planning the second day of the second meeting

During the first day I had relied mainly on choosing a low-threat topic, about which all four presidents knew a good deal and which was relatively simple to discuss in concrete terms. The 'concrete' nature of our discussion was maintained, and if anyone expressed an idea or a 'theory', it was not difficult for me to bring them back to the facts with a question like: 'But how do you do it? Are you involved personally, or is it the salesman?' 'Could you give me an example that illustrates your theory?' etc. Thus, in this respect the day had been successful.

My other goals for this meeting had been to increase the amount of information generated, to reduce the risk of line–staff conflict, and to assuage the competition between the presidents. In order to diminish the risk of a line–staff conflict and to

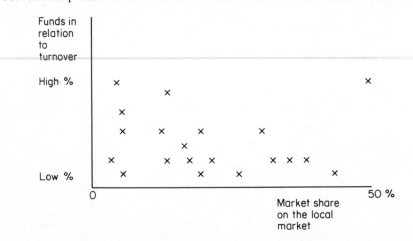

Figure 6.4. E's model, plotting the member companies

neutralize potential competition, I planned during the second day to try to make all the members aware of the structural properties of the group. I also wanted to try to strengthen my personal relationship with the individual presidents.

I was still very anxious to get the individual group members to contribute more to the common pool of information. I had realized that certain structural elements in the organization and the group appeared to be inhibiting the search for new information, and I was therefore determined to try to find some way of bringing out into the open all the values and knowledge which, although perhaps latent, were already available in the group. I had planned to do this chiefly by getting the participants to analyse a particular problem area, and to repeat the analysis using different models requiring different types of data. I hoped that this would also make it possible for me to start tentatively questioning some of the established beliefs of the organization.

The second day of the second meeting

The second day of the second meeting opened with E's presentation of a price-setting model (developed by E and myself as a basis for discussing present pricing policies). The model was based on the relations between market strength and financial strength; organizational and growth conditions were included as additional constraints.

When E had presented the model (which he considered suitable as an instrument for independent pricing in the different companies, given certain agreed pricing rules), the following discussion took place.

Interventionist: E holds that there is an ideal ratio between market share and financial funds for which all companies should strive.

A: But you all remember what happened in one region a few years ago; it didn't cost a penny for competitor Z to attack, and the board of directors of the company in that region was extremely upset.

E: Yes, but what you say just shows how necessary it is to have a good ratio – but can you tell me what I should do, with my poor ratio? What is the minimum ratio for survival?

D: There isn't one!

A: (simultaneously) You can't establish one!

D: That depends on what happens on the market.

A: Competitor X may never get such an idea.

E: But if I want to go to my board of directors and argue that I want to raise the price by 20% for our biggest consumer category, I must be able to provide strong motives, as the board of directors represents this consumer category!

You (to D) say that I can just give my reasons verbally, but not actually present a ratio . . . .

D: How do you establish the ratio? (Irritated) It doesn't make sense! We just can't make comparisons like this!

B: If we are in a position like the one you suggested, (to E) we have other data that can motivate such a decision.

E: OK, we agree about the goals – but I want to translate this into something operational! Take company F: they must face a situation like this . . . (explains why).

C: But that can't be any problem!

B: He can easily motivate why he wants to raise his prices . . . (explains why).

I concluded that E's pricing model had been perceived as a threat to the independence of the local companies, as it contained a formula for mechanistic pricing decisions that could easily be made by the central organization. The discussion continued and my job was to facilitate communications between E and the four presidents. Eventually I presented another pricing model in order to steer the discussion into other paths. This model represented a special version of oligopolistic pricing. In the subsequent discussion there were no major differences of opinion between the presidents and member E, because there was nothing in this model to threaten or discomfit the presidents.

For the rest of the second day we continued to discuss the material prepared by member E, i.e. the feedback from the first meeting. I observed a general willingness to tighten up the original evaluations and to dismiss some of them (positive or negative) as somewhat irrelevant to both short-run and long-run success. I interpreted this as an effect of the greater openness and boldness that was now prevailing in the group. This impression was later supported by a Bales analysis of the taped discussions.

We continued to work on this analysis for another three meetings, and all the members of the group became increasingly independent of their own key groups; they invented new methods of analysis and assumed responsibility for what we were producing together. In the end the question of new business strategies began to monopolize an increasing amount of our attention.

Alpha: organizational and environmental uncertainty structures

As has been mentioned, the Swedish insurance industry has an oligopolistic structure. This makes competitor reactions highly predictable. The companies in the industry have different profiles as regards markets, value-group affiliations, products etc. A retrospective survey shows that certain patterns seem to have remained fairly stable.

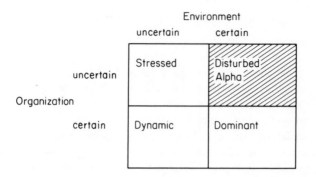

Figure 6.5. Uncertainty structure, Alpha

The owners of the Alpha company were mostly farmers and all the local boards and the top management were recruited among farmers or their organizations. The owners and top executives of the organizations thus tended to hold very similar views about Alpha and its future development. Only one major trade union was likely to have any impact on Alpha's workforce, so here too the company enjoyed stable conditions.

Internally, however, Alpha's situation was not quite so calm and secure. During the assessment phase it had thus emerged that the internal control systems were inadequate to meet changes in demand or competitor behaviour. Further, the organizational culture was characterized by conservatism and defensiveness. The financial resources were very unevenly distributed in the company, and this meant that certain parts of the company were vulnerable to competitive attacks.

In short, the organizational and environmental uncertainty structures of Alpha could be assessed as 'disturbed'.

Further analysis showed that the appropriate coping style for Alpha should focus on the development of internal systems, organizational culture, and resources, rather than on diversification or entrepreneurial development. The following assessment of the organization's strengths and weaknesses was also drawn up by the marketing group.

Strengths and weaknesses of Alpha as evaluated by the marketing group

Alpha's strengths in its present market situation could be summarized in the following points.

Customers considered that:

- Alpha's insurance policies were as good or better than those of its competitors and their premiums were lower.
- Alpha was less bureaucratic than the large international companies, and generally 'easier to deal with'.

Moreover, in comparison with its competitors: Alpha had:

- A large number of customer contacts with private individuals as a result of its big market share of householders' insurance.
- A good many customer contacts in the agricultural sector as well as extensive institutional and ideological connections with this field, as a result of the dominating market share of agricultural insurance and of the company's comprehensive knowledge of agriculture.
- Large number of customer contacts with municipalities, as a result of the high market share of municipal insurances.
- Better contact with local decision-makers, partly as a result of the composition of the board.
- Better knowledge of local conditions as a result of the geographically organized system of representatives and the locally recruited staff.
- More efficient local organization as a result of the board's and the managing director's overall right of decision and economic responsibility.
- More flexible organization and opportunities for quick decisions as a result of officials' greater responsibility.
- More informal forms of cooperation, and a staff with greater motivation.
- Better selection of customers and risks.
- Better control system for evaluation of customers and risks.

Alpha's weaknesses in the present market situation could be summarized in the following points.

Customers considered that:

- Alpha's resources were less adequate for coping with complex insurance arrangements – for large companies, for example.
- Alpha's limited geographical area of operations made it more difficult for the company to provide competitive insurance packages and service to firms and organizations operating also outside this area.

Furthermore, in comparison with its competitors (the national companies) Alpha had:

- A diminishing customer base in its largest and most important customer category – the farmers.
- Less capital resources of its own.
- No ideological or institutional contact with any other customer category except the farmers.
- An incomplete range.
- Not all the necessary specialist functions within its own local organization.
- Less opportunity for staff promotion, and a smaller 'reserve capital' in its personnel and organization.
- Fewer resources for administrative routines and product development.

The strengths and weaknesses listed here, together with the assessment of uncertainty structures and the preliminary analysis of the group, provided the basis for the market strategy presented below. More stress was laid on developing the strengths than on remedying the weaknesses. To a great extent the lack of resources and capacity was rectified by Alpha's membership of the association and the association's wholly owned service company. Before examining the opportunities in greater detail, certain restrictions on growth should first be mentioned.

Restrictions on growth

The following circumstances appear to have represented restrictions on growth.

Households

In view of competitor P's strong foothold in certain towns, any increase in the market share for tenant householders' insurance there could be expected to precipitate reactions on the part of P. In some other places it should be possible to expand operations with this type of customer in mind without causing any competitive reactions.

On the national plane the notable expansion of the provincial insurance companies in the customer category 'one-family households' and 'two-family households' had been causing irritation among the major competitors. If Alpha increased its market share significantly in this segment, confrontation with competitors was to be expected.

Agriculture

The national companies regarded the farmers as Alpha's natural customers and it was not expected that they would institute any measures to attract the farmers provided Alpha did not continue to increase its market share among other types of customer. A certain amount of confrontation with the small local and district companies could be expected from any such activities on the part of Alpha.

Companies and municipalities

The agricultural associations were mainly insured with competitor X, competitor Y, and Alpha. Some selective expansion would be possible without arousing competitive reactions, since the other competitors regarded agriculture as Alpha's special sphere of interest.

Expansion of a selective kind among small companies was not expected to trigger off any competitive reaction.

The municipalities were insured mainly with Alpha or competitor Y. If Alpha were to upset this balance, considerable irritation was to be expected on the part of Y.

If Alpha tried to increase its market share in the apartment house sector, reactions could also be expected, mainly from Y. However, a certain amount of expansion might pass unnoticed in certain selected places.

Consolidation

Alpha's degree of consolidation (shareholders' capital in relation to total premiums) had dropped from 140 to 93 during the market expansion of the previous four years.

Alpha's consolidation was very good in comparison with that of its competitors. However, its relatively small volume of business called for a much higher degree of consolidation than was necessary in the large national companies. In relation to other provincial insurance companies, Alpha's degree of consolidation was relatively low. The company needed to increase its capital resources in order to maintain its freedom of action.

Profitability

Alpha's profitability had been satisfactory in recent years. Profitability should not fall below the 1971 level.

Organization

The number of employees had risen over the last five years. The organization was now big enough to cope with single cases of illness or holiday without any serious disturbance in day-to-day routines.

Communications and cooperation in the company were informal and easy, and the level of service was good.

Invention

In the invention phase meetings occurred more frequently than in the assessment phase. Talks were also often held between certain members of the group and one or more specialist non-members. Problem-solving became more specific, and questions of implementation and acceptability gradually began to occupy more of our attention.

My goals and plans for the invention phase

In the invention phase I felt that the most urgent task was to analyse the data and descriptions agreed upon in the group during the assessment phase, and to generate ideas for further action. In this new phase, therefore, it would be a question of combining existing data in new ways rather than searching for fresh data. As a group we should now try to agree upon specific analytical models to help in the choice of future policies and we should learn together how to use these models. We also had to try to agree on the policies themselves.

To begin with member E, with his broad practical knowledge of the insurance industry, and I, with my experience of theoretical model building and problem-solving, were to work together on the design of models relevant to strategy foundation in the insurance industry as a whole and in this organization in particular. We also decided that if possible we should call in such specialists from the central organization as were appropriate to the particular areas we were discussing. Finally, we planned to encourage interaction between the marketing group and other members of the organization, so as to enrich the group and avoid isolating it from other executives.

Improving group and organizational dynamics

The group members were now communicating more freely and efficiently and did not appear to feel any hesitation about asking for clarifications, suggesting ideas, or revealing their hunches. They also frequently expressed their opinions – positive or negative – about particular ways of approaching the various problems. For this reason questions of group dynamics no longer seemed so crucial.

Numerous meetings were held, attended by two or three members of the group and specialists from other functional areas of the central organization. Member E and I met frequently, often at short notice, whenever one of us had some idea we wanted to discuss. Formal group meetings were devoted to the critical examination of any propositions suggested by the members. E frequently contacted other individual members, to check certain facts before the formal meetings, and one or other of the company presidents sometimes contacted E to discuss regional developments. Policies and priorities agreed in the group were often revised as new policies were analysed. Finally, various subproblems that had already been solved were reconsidered, as new problems came up for scrutiny. There was no formal decision-making, but agreement among group members about the organization's strategy was growing throughout this phase. The group became more open in its interaction with the environment, and various exchange processes with the environment assumed greater importance than before.

Throughout the period during which the marketing group was busy formulating its strategy, various computer-based information systems were being developed in Alpha. Formal and informal meetings, in which E participated, were being held on this subject in the central organization. E wanted the systems-development people to use the general ideas proposed by the marketing group as a basis for the development of the information systems. The systems people, on the other hand, felt that the marketing group should specify exactly what type of information they wanted in the shape of a 'list of operational demands'. However, the marketing group was not yet ready to be so specific; nor had they obtained a consensus for their ideas on such questions as priorities and policies in the rest of the organization. A special information-systems group was formed; E and I were invited to attend together with several systems people and the administrative director.

Many ideas were floated, but we were unable to reach much agreement; it was even difficult to find a common language. The systems people wanted detailed instructions from the marketing side about the kind of feedback most urgently required for efficient market planning. E and I, on the other hand, wanted to get a consensus decision on certain principles for the information system; for instance we wanted to discuss the construction of a decentralized system to supply the autonomous companies, rather than the central organization, with relevant information. The group met a few times and the systems people stated their ideas, and E and I stated ours. E and I were certainly influenced by their way of putting the questions, although we were not yet prepared to make definite statements. The systems people also admitted in the end that they understood our point of view, but did not see what they could do about it. Finally we all realized that no specific agreement was possible at that stage of our respective projects. We agreed to keep in touch regularly and to exchange ideas, and decided that at a later stage we would probably be able to design workable solutions on a more operational level.

Another example of interaction with the intraorganizational environment appeared in the group's various contacts with the product departments. The production people naturally saw the products as the starting point of any analysis of market relations, whereas the marketing group had chosen the customer and market segments as their starting point. These different ways of looking at the organization and its markets gave rise to different vocabularies, different analytical models, and different ideas about profitability. No specific solutions were found to any of these conflicts, but the marketing group agreed to reformulate some of their ideas to make them seem more convincing and acceptable to the production people.

These two examples may suffice to illustrate how the group became involved in ongoing operations, and what impact these involvements had on their own work. The group also began to see some of its ideas being implemented in concrete situations and being accepted by some of the key executives in the organization. The fact that the group members were all involved in current operations – each in his own organizational context – was of course of the utmost importance; it not only made it easier to get reactions from the organization but it also made it possible to influence the organization in a way that would eventually smooth the path for easier acceptance of the marketing strategy.

As had been mentioned, interaction with the environment was now becoming increasingly important. For some products and in some market segments profits had been low for most of Alpha's competitors during 1971–2. However, Alpha was not engaged to any great extent in just these segments, so their profitability had been more favourable. Partly as a result of their low profitability, the three biggest competitors had recently lowered the quality and raised the price of certain of their products. The marketing group was now studying these competitors' actions and the implications that they might have on the market. Member E, as director of marketing, was in daily contact with any member companies who needed his advice on the best way of responding to the competitors' actions. While all this was happening I kept in regular contact with E, and with some of the company presidents, to discuss price and product behaviour in an oligopoly market. We based our talks on cases from other industries and the new data we had been collecting. Naturally the company presidents, too, were all considering ways of reacting to the new market situation. This product–price problem prompted the group to repeated revision of pricing policies, and these continuous exchanges with the extraorganizational environment certainly had an impact on group thinking.

Many other examples of extraorganizational events – shifts in consumer attitudes, mass-media interventions, government policies, other actions on the part of competitors and so on – could be mentioned, but the above examples may perhaps suffice to illustrate the kind of relations that developed between the group and its extraorganizational environment during the evaluation phase.

During the invention phase the involvement of experts in certain questions, the exchange of ideas, and the interpretation of various events together with other executives, as well as the group's involvement in current operations, successively changed the character of the group-environment exchange processes. These processes no longer consisted of the somewhat passive collection of information from the environment; instead they now implied a real involvement in organizational activities, which gave the group new insights into the norms and values obtaining in the organization. With this active involvement, the group also became an increasingly powerful key group in the organization.

During the invention phase there were thus changes in the roles of all the group members, including my own. The company presidents grew more active in all kinds of ways. They were compelled to act when their own companies were involved (e.g. in connection with the pricing decisions exemplified above); on other occasions they alone were able to provide certain information that was essential to E's consideration of some specific current problem (e.g. the development of the information systems). In all these ways our discussion of policies and principles was enriched by events in the surrounding world. The continuous feedback from the environment stimulated the group to tackle specific concrete issues and orientated it more firmly towards *action*, as its members experienced in everyday decision-making the problems that it was currently examining.

My role also changed during this phase. Group members began to use me as an expert on market behaviour and policy formation; it was also useful for them to have access to someone like myself who knew a certain amount about their organization and who was familiar with some of the relevant theories, but who was not involved in current operations in the same way that they were. As one of the company presidents put it: 'I can pass the ball to you, and get it back again.

This helps me to clarify what I'm thinking and doing.' Or, as E often said: 'I'm just calling you to check my own ideas on this . . . ' I no longer felt I had to make any specific effort to activate the group; the initiative now generally came from the various members themselves.

When I subjected the tape recordings of our meetings to a Bales' analysis, I found that communication patterns now embraced all group members much more evenly, and I noted that when any sort of controversial subjects came up for discussion, the participants said what they thought and argued about their opinions before gradually coming to agreement on a common stand.

Invention of a new business strategy

The invention of new ways of approaching problems and new ways of approaching one another had proved extremely important to the marketing group. It had become possible for group members to exchange ideas and discuss intentions more openly among themselves and with other members of the organization. It had also become possible for them to reach agreement on the formulation of a business strategy for the company.

In order to maintain the decentralized structure and to allow for the varied conditions under which each company operated, the strategy was written for a 'model' company, which was nevertheless referred to as 'Alpha'. The following is an abstract of the written strategy.

The actual strategy document was not perhaps the most important invention or 'product' of the group's joint task. The most significant result of its work was rather the perpetual intervention of its members in various ongoing processes in the organization.

Nevertheless the following formal statements were important, since some of the values that had been among the most controversial were now given clear and unambiguous expression by this important key group.

Market strategy

In view of the strengths and weaknesses listed above and the notable quantitative expansion of the last few years, and in view of the profitability trends and restrictions on growth, Alpha should go in for carefully planned expansion.

In the first place Alpha should concentrate on qualitative expansion and reinforce its present market position by focusing on present customers and by developing total insurance services to these customers, with special emphasis on the farmers.

Second, Alpha should try to improve profitability by developing and improving the processes of risk evaluation.

Third, Alpha should expand selectively into certain new markets.

Alpha should also improve administrative routines, invest in personnel development, and increase its return on capital.

The above measures should provide better opportunities for meeting new customer requirements and answering competitive attack.

Behaviour vis-à-vis competitors

Alpha wants to remain a fairly small, local customer-owned insurance company, known for specializing on certain categories of customer. This calls for a particular pattern of behaviour vis-à-vis competitors.

Alpha's market situation and strategic behaviour on the property insurance market can be usefully compared with the circumstances and activities of a guerilla band. The guerilla uses short decision paths and its decisions are made quickly. It lives on its superior knowledge of local conditions and the local population, which means that it can act more promptly, more inventively, and often more efficiently than its larger and wealthier opponents.

- By striving to be consistently superior to its competitors in the eyes of certain customer categories, and by giving these customer/owners the best service while also maintaining institutional and ideological relations with them, Alpha should be able to create barriers of such strength that competitors will be discouraged from trying to force them.
- Alpha should seek direct confrontation with major competitors only when it comes to retaining an important customer category. If Alpha is exposed to competitive attack in any of its main customer or product areas, it should reply by attacking the competitor in a customer or product area that is particularly important to the competitor concerned. Otherwise Alpha should try to achieve its goals without challenging competitor organizations unnecessarily.
- Alpha should not exploit to the full any expansion opportunities that may occur. The company should maintain an organization that is flexible enough, and funds that are substantial enough, to allow its standing and its profile to survive any possible short-term premium reductions or reductions in sums insured.
- Alpha should aim to exploit its knowledge of local conditions: the company should be able to respond to changes in demand by maintaining more flexible pricing, service, and information systems than its competitors; it should also be possible for Alpha to choose the customers who are the most favourable in terms of risk.

Choice of customer categories

Households

Alpha should not invest resources in increasing its market share of tenant households in apartment blocks.

The investments over the last few years in household insurance for one-family and two-family homes in small and medium-sized communities has given Alpha a new foothold on the market outside agriculture. Alpha should aim to maintain its present market share.

Agriculture

In view of the development trends in the insurance industry, the agricultural sector appears to provide Alpha's most important customer category in the long term. In view of this Alpha should aim to be the main insurer and market leader for farmers and related associations.

Despite the risk of confrontations, Alpha should aim to provide insurance for the agricultural associations, which means an increasing investment in resources common to the provincial insurance associations. It also means working to promote the company's ideological and institutional relations with these associations.

Companies and local authorities

Since agriculture is a diminishing segment and expansion in the home-insurance sector should in future be conducted with greater caution, Alpha intends to expand selectively into commercial and small-company insurance. This segment is not as sensitive to possible group-property solutions as, for example, the household market.

Alpha does not regard large-scale industry as belonging to its area of operations.

Many local authorities insure with Alpha. The company should aim to continue to insure the local authorities, and to increase its market share somewhat in this area.

After the outlining of various important points on which the group had recommendations to make (where to grow, where to maintain positions, where to contract, and what general competitive modes to assume), some more detailed policies as regards pricing, products, customer contacts, advertising etc. were suggested.

Realization

As a result of its major work of analysis and its own learning processes, the group had been able to invent new strategies in important domains of the company's operations.

However, although the group had achieved a common standpoint as a result of its long and comprehensive analysis, its members could not yet be sure that the visible outcome of their work — the actual document produced — would communicate their message to other people in the organization. Thus, the general situation at the end of the invention phase was as follows: the group had achieved greater maturity and had developed a strong feeling of group solidarity – it was pleased with the way it had solved problems and reached decisions; but, despite the greater openness attained and the interventions already undertaken by some of its members, the group as a whole was still rather uncertain of itself vis-à-vis its environment, and particularly vis-à-vis some of the other company presidents who might be expected to object to the group's analysis for reasons of prestige, power, envy, or contradictory values.

In the realization phase the group's aim was to gain acceptance for its strategic ideas among those who would have to implement them. This meant finding out what other executives in the organization thought about the content of the plan, probing the values of other important key groups, and at the same time holding the group together in the face of possible criticism or other external pressure; it also meant passing on to each other any feedback received individually from external sources. The group (myself included) now had to decide what action would be necessary for achieving these goals.

My principal plan for the realization phase was to let the group function on its own and only where necessary to help group members with their individual intervention activities. The group agreed to assume responsibility for designing and executing their intervention process, and to use me as a shadow consultant only.

The first group meetings during the production phase were devoted to reading and revising various sections of the written document. Group members all contributed by correcting or rewriting certain passages, and some of the work was also divided between member E and myself.

Once all passages had been subjected to critical revision and verbal analysis, the group checked the various documents for readability and began to communicate their principal ideas to key actors in the organization.

Activities during the realization phase

Each president in the group leads a seminar in his own company

Each president in the group was to hold a seminar in his own company, to present the various ideas and to find out what his subordinates and his board of directors felt about the various issues raised. These opinions were then to be communicated to the group, which would discuss them together.

Presentation to the top executives of the central organization

Top executives in the central organization had been kept continually informed of the group's progress by E and myself, and they had already passed on some of their reactions to E. Thus, when they now looked through the documents, it was mainly to discuss particular words and expressions which could be expected to have some specific impact. This was regarded by the group as a useful check on the readability of the documents.

Visit to another organization

The group decided to accept an invitation (without my participation) to a seminar to be held in another country in an insurance company with an organizational and customer structure similar to Alpha's. It was felt that this would be a good opportunity to discuss certain crucial ideas in the written document, thus getting some feedback from an external, neutral, and well-informed source.

Presentation to the executives of the marketing department

The executives in the marketing department had not seen any previous manuscripts or drafts of the documents. Their involvement had been restricted to providing expert assistance in the solving of certain specific problems during the evaluation phase. Their comments were thus felt to be very important, since they were the people responsible for providing the various staff services that would be necessary to the efficient implementation of the strategy as a whole.

Reactions to the product

The activities of the realization phase were designed by the group without much help from me. The question of presenting the strategic ideas to the rest of the organization – selling them, as E put it – had been discussed from time to time at all stages in the project. It was not thus surprising that all the members of the group now had various ideas of their own on this subject. When one member announced that he was going to hold a seminar with the board of directors in his own company, to get their reactions and to exert some influence on them, the other company presidents announced similar plans of their own. The seminar reports that I subsequently received spoke of a generally positive acceptance of the plan and mentioned the reformulation of certain passages in the document to avoid possible misinterpretation.

The report that I received of the group's trip abroad contained a fairly detailed section explaining why the foreign organization had been unable to understand some of our choices and evaluations. But on the whole the group returned full of enthusiasm over the opportunity provided for airing some of their trickiest problems with the top executives of a similar organization.

When E presented the document to the executives of the marketing department, I was present. Most of the questions raised concerned the way the document was to be used by the member companies, and what specific impact certain ideas could be expected to have on current operations in the marketing department of the central organization. The general ideas contained in the document were already familiar to the executives as a result of their daily interactions with member E, who was of course their boss.

The presentation to the presidents and chairmen of all the regional companies was generally regarded as a success. The group members enacted a lively replay of some of their own earlier discussions of topics which seemed particularly appropriate to the present context.

The regional seminars were regarded by group members as a crucial test of the validity of their document. Would it succeed in communicating vital strategic ideas in a way that was convincing, acceptable, and relevant to the participants? For my part, I saw these seminars as the ultimate test of the validity of my intervention. The programme planned for all four seminars worked well. There was plenty of discussion, conflicting views of the various strategic ideas were brought out into the open and, on the whole, the principal recommendations of the marketing group were accepted. My function at these seminars was to act as an external expert on marketing and business policy. Sometimes I introduced relevant theories and models as a basis for discussions in small groups, and sometimes I summed up by presenting some more general ideas on the topics discussed in these groups and in the plenary sessions. Formally, E led the seminars. Now and then he supplied information or filled in some of the background to various actions on the part of competitors or to other market events.

Once the seminars were over, most companies proceeded to internal discussion of the various strategic issues raised by the group's document or by participants at the regional seminars. At this point the marketing group agreed that its task was finished, and I regarded my intervention as over. I withdrew from the project and from my role in the organization.

New projects had been generated by the strategy formulation project, and these were now leading to the establishment of groups similar to the original marketing group. Adjustments and reformulations continued to be made in the various member companies of the organization.

Formal decision and realization of the new business strategy

By the time the formal decision was taken at the board of the joint association, the new strategy was already in use. Most company presidents had internalized its principles and were busy developing an individual company strategy adapted to their respective organizational and market conditions. Thus, with the behavioural and development approach that we had chosen, implementation of the product was built into the learning and change process. This probably contributed to the success that Alpha enjoyed on the market throughout the remainder of the 1970s.

Epilogue

The strategy designed by the marketing group continued to be adjusted and developed over the years. Structural modifications were implemented and the focus of attention shifted gradually from strategic and marketing problems to administrative systems and production technology.

The marketing director, E, became president of one of the largest and most powerful member companies, a position which he still held in 1981. The other members of the group, i.e. the company presidents, also occupied the same positions in 1981 as they had held at the time of the project.

CHAPTER 7

An Experiential IDS – The Beta Case

Synopsis

In this chapter we will describe an intervention in a corporate development process. The first step in this assignment consisted of an inquiry into the means of control and the internal relations prevailing in the client organization. As a result of the initial assessment of internal relations, attention came to focus on an assessment of organizational and environmental structures. These two assessment processes led to the invention of new strategies and new norms for control and communications, which were subsequently implemented in the organization.

The organization operates in the wood industry. It consists of a holding company and a number of saw mills, trading companies, and plants for the manufacture of building components. In the following pages we will refer to the organization as Beta, or sometimes as the group (of companies).

The intervention described below is also an example of IDS, but the actions involved were not the same as those we have just examined in Chapter 6. The intervention did not for instance start with our participating in a group decision process. Instead we embarked on a series of analysis-and-feedback cycles, in the course of which we penetrated the various problems ever more deeply; subsequently our discoveries about behavioural processes led to other discoveries regarding strategic problems; these in turn led to inventions and, ultimately, to the implementation of the products of the process, or what we have called 'realization'.

This intervention, partly on account of its different design, involved us in aspects of both behaviour and strategy that had no part in the insurance company case. But the Beta case resembled Alpha in that some of our intervention actions may have had consequences we never intended.

Background to the Assignment and a Description of the Organization

Beta was founded by two large Swedish companies in the forest industry in 1975; its aim was to grow and to earn money from the acquisition of successful and expanding small family-owned companies. The first such company was bought in 1975, and by 1978 Beta consisted of the holding company and eight subsidiaries.

Beta was wholly owned by the two large companies, and one of its original goals had been to grow without involving the small flexible subsidiaries in the administrative systems of the owner companies. Another aim, which had been expressly acknowledged from the outset, was that the owner companies should learn something of the mechanisms by which small family-owned companies can remain successful and profitable even in periods of economic strain.

From the very beginning in 1975–6 the managing director of Beta made it quite clear to the subsidiary managers that decision-making was to be highly decentralized, and that they – the managers – were to enjoy considerable independence. None the less several events occurred during 1976 which according to the subsidiary managers had greatly curtailed their companies' freedom of action. During 1977 and 1978 this trend became even more marked. Money was borrowed against the subsidiaries' guarantee but without their agreement; a central marketing executive was appointed without previous consultation with the subsidiaries; a central and unilateral decision was made about the companies' group contributions for 1977. All these actions were regarded by the subsidiary companies as signs of growing centralization.

Apart from these major events, we were also told that the way in which the central unit passed on information and issued directives to the subsidiary companies added to the impression that an overcentralized bureaucracy was taking over.

Three of the subsidiary managers, worried about these developments, had complained to the chairman of the board, criticizing the way the managing director was running operations. A whole series of central decisions had so curtailed their freedom of action that they no longer felt they could be held responsible for their own companies' results. They also wondered openly whether the managing director was sticking to the original agreements which had emphasized their independent status.

Assessment

Our first analysis of relations in Beta

First, in an attempt to probe more deeply into the problems of the group, and so that we could tell the clients how *we* would describe *their* problems, we interviewed executives and union representatives in the subsidiaries and top executives in the holding company. The following is the survey we produced, based on our findings.

Strategic decisions

Product and market decisions involving minor changes and requiring no investment were generally made by the respective subsidiary companies.

Decisions regarding big investments or extensive market investigations came up before the board of the relevant subsidiary. The opinion of the company chairman, i.e. the managing director of the group, thus generally prevailed, particularly if any really large investments were involved.

In 1977 a central marketing function was established. Its main task was to coordinate the marketing operations of the subsidiary companies. Since then a clear trend towards central decision-making had been noted, even on questions of minor strategic importance or of a purely operational nature.

The financing of development (and other) investment was decided by the boards, and again the chairman's view almost always carried the day. Funds for investment were often taken from one company and used in another.

In other words, since decisions on strategic developmental issues were generally regarded as matters for the company boards, and since the managing director of Beta was chairman of all the boards, the deciding voice was his. According to the company managers he was not prepared to discuss any conflicting ideas.

Certain administrative and operational marketing decisions were also becoming increasingly centralized. For example, as we have seen, a central marketing function had been established, and more frequent as well as more detailed reporting was now being demanded.

Methods for operational planning and control

Since the establishment of Beta, a budget system had been developed and the same procedures were now followed in all the subsidiary companies. On a basis of the monthly reports and the four-monthly accounts, the central unit was able to keep a regular and detailed check on budget outcomes. Thus an effective tool had evolved for steering and controlling operations, although so far it did not seem to have been used very much for this purpose; rather, it had become an element in the subsidiaries' own planning.

In the present organization the operational management of production and sales was decentralized.

Forms of communication between parent company and subsidiaries

Since the managing director of the group was also the chairman of all the subsidiary boards, board meetings came to represent an important link in communications between the parent company and its subsidiaries. According to the local managers, the managing director was inclined to dominate these meetings, and they felt that too much time was spent discussing operational planning and the details of economic reporting; no time was left for any serious discussion of the future of the subsidiaries, or of future strategies and relations between parent and subsidiaries. At the same time the managers never quite dared to tell the managing director that they were dissatisfied with the situation.

Information from the subsidiaries to the parent company consisted mainly of economic reporting. Information from the parent company to the subsidiaries often took the shape of standardized letters to the local managers containing fairly detailed instructions about the way they were to act in negotiating agreements, arranging study trips, preparing their economic reporting, and so on.

While the system of economic planning and follow-up was being developed, there had been frequent contact and a good deal of information exchange between the central finance department and the subsidiaries. Most of the subsidiaries had found this personal contact and joint problem-solving to be a positive and constructive experience, although many people suspected that the real purpose of the meetings was to pave the way for even greater centralization.

Quality of relations between parent company and subsidiaries

Generally speaking the relationship between the subsidiaries and the parent company were marked by *mistrust* rather than mutual confidence, *manipulation* rather than open confrontation and conflict-solving, and the *control of details* rather than the discussion of goals.

The *mistrust* revealed by the managing director in his relations with subordinates showed itself in the detailed 'hearings' about budgets and outcomes to which, as chairman of the boards, he subjected his subsidiary managers; in the personal interviews he held with applicants for sales appointments; in the decisions he made over the heads of the local managers when any major sum of money was involved; and in the detailed instructions he issued about agreements, etc. The subsidiary companies, on their part, showed their mistrust of the central unit in a tendency to discern secret 'centralistic' motives even where there were none.

When changes were being made, there was often evidence of manipulation. For example, when a marketing function was being established to coordinate the marketing operations of the subsidiary companies, everything was decided centrally without any consultation with the companies actually concerned. And when an extensive system of operational control and follow-up was being designed, it was actually introduced as a perfectly innocent information system; practically nothing was said about the opportunities it implied for controlling and steering operations down to the very last detail.

At the same time the subsidiary managers took every opportunity that came their way of bypassing the boards and avoiding the necessity of reporting vitally important events or decisions. Thus they often reported comparatively insignificant operational details, but kept quiet about things that really mattered – all with a view to maintaining as much independence as possible. This sort of behaviour naturally reinforced the parent company's lack of trust; it also provoked further manipulations and encouraged a general fixation on unimportant details.

First feedback to the board of directors

These findings were reported to the board of directors of Beta and to the managing director. Nobody seemed particularly upset and the managing director acted most cooperatively, probably because of his very delicate position.

One board member asked us what we thought might be the cause of the problems, and we then suggested that a gap existed between the company's espoused (overtly declared) strategies and the norms and strategies actually prevailing.

At this stage we made a more detailed comparison between the espoused theories of organization and control (as agreed between the managing director and the subsidiaries when the group was originally created) and the way things were actually being run according to our interview data.

To illustrate our point we presented two ideal types of control and organization; one we called the *flexibility model* and the other the *synergy model*. We argued that in most public statements in Beta the flexibility model was espoused; it was this model which was supposed to provide a norm for control and organization. None the less, in most of the major actions and decisions of the holding company, as far as we could see from our data, the goal was to reap the benefits of large-scale production, financing, or marketing, to exert control over operations with the help of administrative systems, and to acquire an overview on which rational top management decisions could be based.

In order to reveal the nature of the conflict, we described and explained the two ideal types as below.

Decisions, responsibility, and control in the synergy model

The synergy model is based on the assumption that an organization's efficiency is best promoted by exploiting the economy of large batches, by developing narrow but highly qualified specialist functions, by evolving quick and effective systems of information and control, and by utilizing various synergy effects (on the market by bringing together products with similar customer and buyer structures, in manufacturing by bringing together products that lend themselves to similar techniques, and in administration and financing by the introduction of standard procedures).

In the synergy model the overriding strategic responsibility for results is centralized, while specific operational responsibility for results is decentralized. Sources of funds, types of markets and products, and development strategy – in other words all the components of corporate strategy – should be decided centrally, while as far as possible the development of specific business strategies and the implementation of marketing programmes, sales, and production should be decided in the various units, subject to the appropriate overview of the central organization.

Decisions, responsibility, and control in the flexibility model

The flexibility model is based on the assumption that efficiency is promoted by making decisions where the job is to be done, by minimizing the distance between decision-makers and between production and markets, and by developing a team which as a result of personal proximity and independence is able and eager to assume responsibility for its own actions. The feeling of being in command at the local level is given priority over the possible benefit of a central overview.

In a flexible and situation-orientated organization, moreover, errors can be promptly discovered and corrected on the spot. The important point is that the decentralized or local unit has complete control over all controllable decision parameters that affect its own results.

The role of the central unit is to evaluate the local units on a basis of their results, to replace any local management which persistently fails to achieve the superordinate goals, to give advice and support in various specialized functions (ideally for a fee), and to help on the financing side. The central unit is also responsible for selling local units which for some reason are or have become unsuited to the type of operations required, and to buy new units where appropriate.

Because of their independent status, their decision-making obligations, and their total responsibility for results, the local units in an organization based on the flexibility model are less secure than they would be under the synergy model. If things go badly in a synergy-orientated organization, there is no saying definitely whether the fault lies with the central strategic decisions or with the local operational people. In the flexibility model the local units always bear all the responsibility and have to accept the consequences of their actions in full.

The control function in the flexibility model and the synergy model

In the synergy model control is exercised by a successive breaking down of goals and strategies into action programmes, budgets, and monthly or weekly plans. The most important control tool is the budget. In budgeting, the breakdown and build-up processes are very important. On the one hand the budget should reflect certain aspects of corporate strategy, while on the other it represents a commitment on the part of the local operational unit. Operations are controlled by means of regular budget follow-ups, and the first requirement of operational responsibility is that budget commitments should be met.

In the flexibility model the main component of central control lies in choosing the operational units which are to belong to the organization (e.g. the buying or selling of subsidiaries). Further, the central unit has a major say in choosing the leaders of the local units, for example the boards and managers of the subsidiary companies. Once these two choices have been made, result trends provide continual grounds for central review. Intermittent control is exercised by the central unit for providing various kinds of information and exerting a certain amount of personal influence. However, although central management can influence the management of a subsidiary by issuing information about market trends, political decisions, expected cost developments, and so on, the local management (which is after all assessed exclusively on its results) is entirely responsible for deciding whether or not to follow the proffered advice.

Reactions at the board meeting

The board of directors consisted of the managing directors and two other representatives of the two owner companies, two managers from other companies in other industries, representatives of the trade union, and the managing director of the Beta group. When we had explained our view of the nature of the conflict in the organization, and had talked about the gap we suspected between espoused norms and strategies and the way things were actually being done, a general discussion of management theory took place. Our 'ideal types' seemed to arouse more interest than our message about the discrepancies between espoused and actual norms. The managing director of one of the owner companies was particularly interested in speculating about the suitability of one or the other model for corporations in general and for his own particular company.

At first, the other owner-company managing director, who was also chairman of the group board, was benevolently disposed towards our findings, but he became increasingly ironical about the theoretical discussion launched by his presidential colleague.

To bring the discussion back to Beta and its problems, one of us asked whether the board had confidence in the group's managing director despite the obvious mistrust he aroused in the managers of the subsidiaries.

The chairman then asked us and the managing director of the Beta group to leave the room, so that the board could discuss the matter and decide on an answer.

An hour later the chairman called the managing director back and issued the following statement: 'This board has full confidence in you as managing director ... and the organization should henceforth be run according to the flexibility model. However, every effort should be made to ensure collaboration between the companies in the group so as to exploit the advantages of joint action in marketing, production, financing etc.' With this statement the case was closed and our consultant contract terminated.

Further analysis and the first feedback seminar

The managing director of the group contacted us a few days later. How, he asked us, would we describe his mandate to run the company? Our advice, in brief, was as follows.

1. As the board had confirmed its confidence in him, he should manage the company as he thought fit.
2. As the board had advocated the adoption of both the flexibility and the synergy models, and since these two models cannot in our view be successfully applied simultaneously, it was up to him to choose between them.
3. Whatever norms and strategies he decided to follow, he should make his choice known and declare openly what stance he had assumed.
4. Whatever position he had adopted, he should be prepared to discuss his

policies and declarations with other people and to listen to any criticisms they might have.

Many long discussions followed, in the course of which the managing director explained what he wanted to do and what he wanted to achieve; but he added that his ambitions did not fit exactly into either of our ideal models. We pointed out that our discussion of ideal types was simply meant to clarify certain aspects of organization, but that the complex task of management in a real-world setting cannot easily be reduced to any such clear-cut patterns.

At further meetings with us the managing director began to expound his views more explicitly, and they proved to be closer to the synergy than to the flexibility model. One reason he gave for this was that he wanted to change the systems of marketing, sales, administration, and production in order to adapt to new market conditions. At this point he asked us to elaborate on our conception of the dynamic market-orientated (as opposed to the production-orientated) company.

We promised to do so, and suggested that he should assemble some of his general managers and other staff for a two-day seminar on the subject. He agreed, but added that the relationship between himself and the others ought first to be discussed and clarified. We decided that a discussion of this problem should be based on our feedback, just as our talks with the board had been, and we fixed a one-day seminar with the subsidiary managers to discuss human relations in Beta.

At this seminar, which was held a couple of days later, the participants confirmed our findings and agreed to go on trying to straighten things out. Most of the general managers said they would take active steps to work out new modes of collaboration, while two insisted that the only problem was the group managing director and that the adoption of the flexibility model was all that was needed.

At this point the managing director gave a clear and detailed exposition of his own ideas, according to which all potential synergy effects should be exploited to produce a dynamic and market-orientated corporation.

Toward new assessments at a series of seminars

A working committee consisting of the managing director and six of the subsidiary managers was appointed, so that work on an experiential IDS could be pursued. The committee was to meet regularly with us, and together we were to probe the possible causes of Beta's problems and to look for ways of dealing with them.

We suggested that a start could be made by exploring some of the most urgent marketing problems. Two managers then mentioned pricing policies as a suitable opener, since these had always been a controversial issue.

After a lengthy discussion two facts emerged.

1. As soon as it was a question of any really sophisticated marketing activities, the managing director of Beta mistrusted the capability of the subsidiaries.

2. The prices of all products were determined in the same way, using a conventional cost-plus pricing method.

These two revelations seemed trivial, and were not in fact revelations at all since everybody already knew the facts. Nevertheless these assessments conflicted with official (or espoused) company policy, according to which 'The subsidiaries are the backbone of our marketing strategy, and their marketing competence and flexibility represents one of the major strengths of the group', and 'Price policies are to be worked out in negotiations between the central unit and the subsidiaries', and further, 'Price should be considered as one parameter in the total marketing mix, and different pricing methods and criteria should be used according to the product's position in its life cycle, the role of the product, or the objectives with respect to a particular market segment'.

The discovery of this gap between the pricing system actually in use and the policies that were officially espoused, triggered off a broader-based discussion of the mechanisms revealed: 'Are these differences between what we say and what we do common in other areas and, if so, what effect does this have?'

During the pricing discussion we noted certain mechanisms at work in the members' ways of relating to one another, and we therefore asked whether we might analyse a few behavioural traits. We made transcripts of our tape recordings to provide supporting evidence in our subsequent discussion of the committee's group behaviour.

Our recordings revealed three types of behaviour that were worth commenting on.

1. On several occasions people had concealed certain facts about the profitability of particular products, perhaps by talking about product lines or product groups as a single clump. And the others had let it pass without comment.
2. If someone judged a particular topic to be 'hot' or possibly threatening to one of the others, he played down his own views so as not to upset anyone. For instance, if someone thought that promotion had been incompetently handled, he worded his criticism in cloudy and indirect terms: 'The parameter mix, particularly promotion, has not been too well adjusted to the market segments.'
3. When one of the managers propounded the 'espoused' view of the subsidiaries as being competent, market-orientated, flexible etc., the managing director generally agreed, although this contradicted what he had previously told us of his own views.

When we first revealed this kind of behaviour to the participants, they made jokes about it and tried to play down its importance. But we insisted that these discoveries should be taken just as seriously as, for example, the revelations about pricing procedures. In the end the committee members agreed with us, and immediately embarked on a process of discovering their own interpersonal behaviour in much the same way that they had previously investigated pricing procedures. During this process of discovery they began to reflect on the differences between what they said and what they did when dealing with one another. Previously they had described their interpersonal relations in terms of trust and openness; now, instead, the tapes revealed mistrust, conformity, and defensiveness.

At this point we, the consultants, started comparing the discoveries about pricing and the evaluations of the sales companies with these later discoveries regarding interpersonal behaviour, and we wondered out loud whether the committee's way of behaving reflected attitudes and actions in the organization as a whole. Was pricing behaviour perhaps guided by the same sort of values and norms that characterized various other kinds of interpersonal behaviour?

We returned once again to our earlier analysis and our discussion of the flexibility and synergy models of management. And this time, as a result of examining their own interpersonal behaviour, the committee members found that some of our original feedback began to make sense to them. Their personal experience in the committee of some of the behavioural modes that were also present in the organization, helped them to recognize the existence of these modes. The revelations originally stemming from our reported survey, and which at first had been passively accepted, had now been translated into real experiences and internalized as active discoveries.

Further learning and change over the first six months

During the next five seminars the group analysed present pricing methods, segmentation strategies, product development policies, and promotion strategies. Some major problems were identified.

● Rigid control systems prevented the adaptation of pricing to the particular objectives of the different products; central control contradicted the decentralized pricing principle.
● Segmentation criteria were intuitive and haphazard, rather than being related to variations in customer needs.
● Segmentation strategies (choices and priorities) were based on tradition rather than on any estimation of growth and profitability.
● Product development was geared to production and technology rather than markets.
● Expenditure on promotion was calculated as a percentage of expected sales, and promotion itself was handled by an external agency.

The participants also analysed their own behaviour and were able to project their experiences on to the organization as a whole. They came up with the following chart of the norms that were steering both marketing and interpersonal behaviour in the organization.

- Beta was steeped in *conservatism*; there were emotional ties with old products and product lines, which made it difficult to discontinue any particular product on objective grounds. Similarly, it was difficult to convince a previously successful subsidiary or salesman that sales methods sometimes need changing.

- There was greater emphasis on punishing mistakes in Beta than there was on rewarding success. Sometimes even success was punished, if it had not been achieved by following the accepted norms and policies. Thus a norm advocating *conformity* had evolved, and this discouraged people from taking risks or seeking new opportunities. Another explanation of the prevailing conformism lay in the rigidly hierarchic relationship between the central unit and the subsidiaries. The managing director was anxious to keep control over the subsidiaries; they, in turn, were expected to see that operations followed the plans prescribed. As a result of this overemphasis on control and obedience managers found it expedient to keep everyone in step rather than to encourage creative thinking.

- Opportunities for promotion or other advancement very often depended on the aspirant's possession of some useful knowledge or information. This led to a certain *defensiveness*: people tended to reserve their knowledge for use on special occasions. Important strategic information was often exploited opportunistically rather than being used as a constructive basis for change and development in the company.

- These norms, which generated conservatism, conformism and defensiveness, appeared to be reinforced by rigid systems of control.

Our feedback on discoveries about conservatism

When the committee had completed their description, they asked us to summarize and systematize the general discoveries they had made. We then presented them with the following general picture.

First, it seemed important to reach some understanding of the relation between organizational norms, control systems, and marketing innovativeness. As Beta relied on old methods of marketing, new products had little hope of succeeding. But to promote the success of new products, it was not enough to discover new concepts of marketing or to learn about new methods; it was also necessary to discover ways of changing the cultural climate of the organization and making it more favourable to the sort of risk-taking and individualism and openness that was necessary to any real improvement in marketing processes. We told the committee that in our opinion the most important components in any organizational culture are the norm systems and the control systems, which together influence the innovativeness of the marketing. (See Figure 7.1, as presented to the committee.)

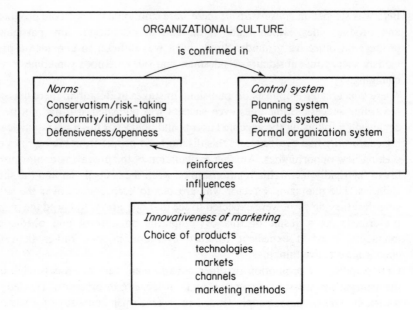

Figure 7.1. Organizational culture and marketing

The static nature of Beta

Beta was at that time confronted with structural changes in competition, technology, and the cost of production factors; it was therefore under great pressure to develop a high degree of innovativeness.

Since the group was steeped in conservatism and conformism, the likelihood of its launching any new products was pretty small. Interest was focused on current products; individual people and the group as a whole tended to identify with present products and present markets. Because of the generally defensive attitude that prevailed, uncomfortable or threatening information – perhaps about failures or disturbing developments on the market – was never brought out into the open and tackled courageously.

The control system reinforced and confirmed the norms, which made it even more difficult to achieve any change. (See Figure 7.2, as presented to the committee.)

If Beta was to succeed in its ambition to launch new products, to explore new market opportunities and to try out new and more unconventional marketing methods, it would have to change its cultural climate as well as its technical competence to handle marketing issues. Thus, in order to succeed, the group needed to become altogether more dynamic. (See Figure 7.3, as presented to the committee.)

In the discussion that followed, our picture became somewhat modified. Several people declared that it was too pessimistic: 'Things aren't really all that bad.' On

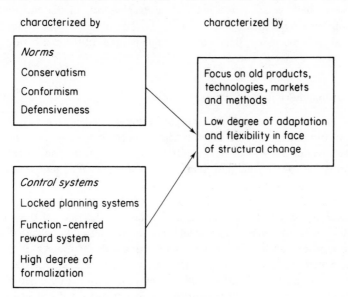

Figure 7.2. The static company

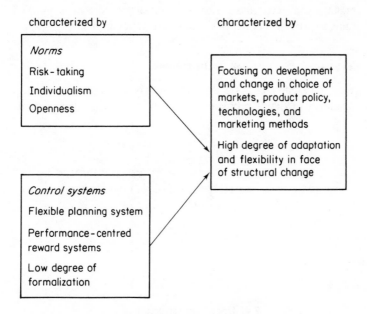

Figure 7.3. The dynamic company

the other hand more evidence emerged that supported our description, and certain facts came to light which made the picture even worse. In the end there was almost complete agreement that, as well as the human relations and other problems already discussed, Beta was in trouble because of the static nature of its organization.

The Beta group under stress

To complement the analysis of Beta's organization we now presented our general typology of organizational and environmental uncertainty structures and coping styles (see Chapter 2). As we checked for general signs of internal uncertainty it became apparent to everyone that Beta was in bad shape. We found a low degree of organizational solidarity, disturbed communication patterns, inadequate control systems, and a low equity ratio – all factors that tend to restrict opportunities for successful development. To this could be added that relations between the owners were problematic and that the various stakeholders disagreed about the kind of development that was now desirable. Moreover, most of the group's products were struggling against extremely unpredictable market conditions due to international disturbances in the pattern of trade in this sector and to political measures in Sweden that restricted house building and reduced demand for the companies' products. These internal and external uncertainties generated considerable stress and called for drastic changes in company operations (see Figure 7.4).

The managing director and the top executives therefore drew up the following programme, to provide a better basis for future action in Beta.

Inventions

By this time the executives in the different parts of the organization had all agreed on the diagnosis of Beta's problems. But there had been little systematic discus-

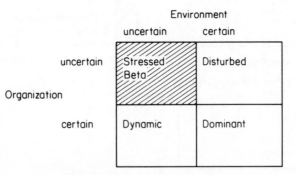

Figure 7.4. Uncertainty structure of Beta

sion as yet about possible ways of putting things right. Several key groups had made various suggestions, among them the following:

1. to reduce the power and resources of the central unit;
2. to increase the power and resources of the central unit;
3. to give the company managers greater independence;
4. to develop more rigorous control and information systems.

And other examples could be given of the diametrically opposite remedies suggested. We claimed that an overriding problem was the lack of any comprehensive corporate strategy and of any business strategies in the subsidiaries. This was the cause of considerable uncertainty; people were not sure what the group was really aiming at. We also pointed out that solutions to present problems should look beyond present operations; they should be worked out in light of a scenario for future operations.

At this point the managing director of the group expounded his own general conception of 'business'. His vision embraced the idea of the 'dynamic company' run on the lines of the synergy model, and he therefore defined the present problems in terms of the gap between this image and operations as they were currently being conducted. Several meetings were held under different forms, and these topics were further discussed. At most of these meetings we were not present.

The following steps (what we have called *inventions*) were eventually agreed upon by various decision units and approved by the board, the managing director, and the subsidiaries.

● The general managers (aged 58 and 60) of two of the companies felt called upon to resign in view of the prevailing circumstances. Two others (of the same age) were replaced against their will.
● Younger professional managers were recruited to replace these four men, and the organization's overall conception of 'business' was clearly explained to them from the outset.
● Projects for the formulation of business strategies were initiated in all subsidiaries. Results were requested within four months.
● An analysis of local and corporate control and information systems was initiated. This too was designed as a quick-action project.
● A business development project for the whole company was launched. This was regarded as a more long-term strategic learning project.
● A series of leader-development seminars was held, at which new management styles were introduced and some modifications in leader behaviour worked out.

Formally, all these decisions were made by Beta's board but the real decisions had been reached earlier in a series of discussions between the managing director and the local managers and between the managing director and ourselves. Some of the more controversial decisions, such as the replacement of the four subsidiary managers, had been agreed informally between the managing director and the chairman.

A new corporate strategy

In response to our comment on the lack of any explicit corporate strategy (which the managing director had agreed to attend to), an executive committee was formed. This group worked intensively for a couple of weeks and the draft of a corporate strategy was produced and accepted by the managers of the subsidiaries.

Corporate strategy 1980–5: a draft

- Beta is to maintain a balanced mix of sawn and planed wood, of building, furniture, and joinery components, of finished products, and of trading business. This is to be achieved in the first place by developing the range of products in the present subsidiary companies and by discontinuing any operations inappropriate to company goals, and in the second place by purchasing companies.
- The choice of products and markets shall be based on an analysis of market needs. A market-orientated planning and manufacturing programme is to be developed. The product and market mix is to be achieved by choosing niches and segments which are appropriate in terms of growth and profitability, and which fit the company's present and potential competence.
- The quantity of sawn and planed standard products is to be reduced in so far as interesting and profitable semi-finished and finished products can be developed.
- In the case of sawn and planed standard products profitability is to be achieved mainly by creating a more efficient distribution system and reducing the distance to the final consumer.
- The quantity of processed wood products is to be increased. These goods shall consist in the first place of components purchased by industrial and building firms or distributors. Special 'unique' products, or products whose patent has been applied for, are also to be favoured.
- In the case of joinery, furniture, and building components, profitability and growth are to be achieved as a result of:

  1. the selective choice of customers;
  2. active 'function' selling;
  3. the adaptation of the manufacturing and marketing organization to the special requirements of the chosen customers;
  4. a combination with certain 'non-wood' products, providing more opportunities for supplying whole systems.

- In the case of packing materials profitability is to be achieved by means of the flexible adaptation of production capacity to prevailing demand conditions and the development of a more efficient distribution structure.
- Opportunities for collaboration between the companies in the group are to lead to better profitability for the organization as a whole, as a result of greater specialization and longer runs. In particular this will involve:

  1. more collaboration within geographically limited areas;
  2. common investment in certain major customer groups and submarkets;
  3. cooperation between companies in the group, where this will advance the group's commercial interests.

- Opportunities for cooperation between companies in the group and raw-material suppliers shall be exploited with a view to improving profitability. In particular this will involve:

  1. choosing products in light of lumber supply and lumber quality in the area;
  2. adjustment of the length and quality of timber products to the requirements of the customer needs;
  3. possible readjustments in the raw material supply to allow for specialization in manufacture.

- By taking an active part in the relevant wood-consumers' trade organizations, and by maintaining contacts with the authorities and the sawmill industry in general, the company should work to improve the structure of the industry and should gradually place less emphasis on wood products and more on components, semi-manufactures and finished products.

Policies

In addition to this general strategic orientation, specific policies were evolved for pricing, distribution, and promotion. One of the fundamental causes of conflict in the past had been the classification of products. The subsidiaries had always felt that specific strategies for the separate product groups would mean more centralization and they had therefore opposed any idea of a systematic classification of products and the development of product strategies. Once the distribution of power in Beta had been openly discussed and clarified, a new approach to the classification of products was no longer a controversial question.

Realization

Development of our consultant role

When we first started working for this client, we were engaged by the managing director and the board to analyse a human relations problem. When we reported back, we focused both on human relations problems and on certain other problems connected with corporate strategy and organizational structure and control.

As a consequence of our first feedback session, several subsequent sessions were also arranged. Gradually our role changed and became more interactive. A series of seminars was held, so that we could discuss the outcome of various research–analysis–feedback cycles concerned with behaviour and policy. In the end we were working more as management advisers and sparring partners than as analysts. The evolution of the consultant–client relationship was reflected in the formal contract: at first we were hired on a project basis, with a budget for each separate project; next we were engaged on a daily basis, without any specific budget; finally we were engaged on a year's contract to participate in a variety of projects and to help to push them ahead.

Replacement of four local managers

From the moment when the decision was reached to replace four of the subsidiary managers, a year was to pass before the new men were all established in their posts. It was a costly year in terms both of money and of human effort and suffering. At this point there was little that we could do to speed up the process. Assessments had been made and the relevant decisions taken; we could only wait.

The two managers who had offered to resign now tried in all sorts of ways to postpone taking the definitive step. And they were fairly successful, since they both had personal and professional connections with powerful members of the owner companies, as well as with the board of the group and the local boards. It began to look as though they had never actually intended to go, but had simply handed in their resignations in a last attempt to get the managing director of the group removed. Eventually they were given other lesser posts within the organization, and one year after the decision date four new and competent managers were established in the subsidiaries, men who were loyal to the now openly acknowledged company strategy. Once these changes had been effected operations soon showed signs of renewed vitality; new and dynamic strategies were launched and there was much discussion about the most effective ways of putting strategies into operation.

Local policy projects

The lack of any explicit or agreed strategies in the local subsidiaries and in the group as a whole had certainly had a negative effect both on marketing and production development and on internal relations. It was therefore felt that the introduction into the subsidiaries of explicit and partly formalized business strategies would improve both effectivenesss and efficiency. There was a good deal of discussion about which should come first, the local business strategies or the overall corporate strategy: to be able to go into specific details in the latter, access was needed to analyses and evaluations from the local companies; on the other hand, might not an overall strategy provide suitable starting points and guidelines for deliberations at the local level? The dilemma was resolved by undertaking both tasks simultaneously and by encouraging frequent interactions between the two. Joint seminars were held on various issues where changes seemed likely or desirable; models were designed for use either in analysis or in strategic choice; and a series of meetings was arranged between the central units and the local company executives so that each side could become familiar with the other's interests, problems, and intentions. It was hoped that this kind of inter-active and open approach to strategy formulation would help to focus plans on the relevant issues and to provide the various analyses with a sounder base; it was also believed that people would feel personally committed to the evaluations and decisions reached and that the whole process would provide a good opportunity for organizational learning and development.

Leader development

Several executives in the various subsidiaries took part in leader-development pro-grammes. The managing director of the group attended a three-day programme with one of us and another consultant. In the course of this programme he was confronted with descriptions of his own behaviour as seen by his subordinates, and on a basis of these descriptions and a few cases of a general character from other leader-development programmes he was able to experiment with alternative ways of dealing with people. He was also able to discuss with the consultants various theories of leadership and leader development as propounded by Argyris (1976), Vroom (1964; 1973), Blake and Mouton (1964), Hersey and Blanchard (1972), Reddin (1970) and others.

The aim of the leader-development seminars was not to induce the executives to change their behaviour, but to help them to become more aware of it and of its impact on others. By helping people to reflect on their own behaviour in this way we hoped to create conditions conducive to change and learning, and by continu-ing to supply feedback and to act in various consultative capacities we hoped to pave the way for more efficient behaviour patterns.

Control systems

Staff specialists in the individual local companies and in the central organization started to work on the revision of the control systems. Their projects were later to be integrated with the strategy projects, to ensure that various indicators of strategy fulfilment could also be subjected to appropriate measurement and control.

Business-development project

One of the most important things to be revealed during the discovery phase was the static and production-centred climate that prevailed in Beta. The analysis of this problem was enriched by the reported facts and by the ideas of the company managers. The owner companies, too, had begun to show growing concern about product and market development.

A project was consequently started to explore ways of earning money by entering new markets or by selling semi-finished products and products more closely adapted to the market. Conventional production and marketing methods were too dominant at present, and active steps to discover the star products of tomorrow seemed called for. As this was too big a project to be run by the subsidiaries, it was undertaken by the central organization together with one of the owner companies.

Epilogue

Beta experienced a number of turbulent changes shortly after the events described above. First, one of the owner companies bought up the other. The new situation encouraged some of the top executives in this company to try to increase their control over the whole group. The managing director took steps to counteract these moves and a struggle for power developed between him and some of the top executives of the owner company.

Following some major structural changes in the Swedish forest industry, the managing director of the owner company resigned to become managing director of one of the other large forest corporations in Sweden. During a period of transition the top management of Beta's owner company was thus in a state of some uncertainty but at the same time it also enjoyed considerable freedom to go its own way.

Shortly after a new managing director had been appointed to the owner company, the managing director of Beta was removed from his post and was not replaced. The group became a division of the owner company.

Despite all these changes the various projects generated by the process of corporate development continued; in fact they were pursued with even greater intensity. The staff of the owner company now became more involved, and as far as the sawmills and the other subsidiaries were concerned, the effects were generally positive. These units all acquired more freedom to develop their own business strategies and to conduct their operations as they thought fit; they also received more support, financial and other, from the group.

As regards the effects of the corporate development project as a whole on market performance, it is still too soon to express an opinion.

CHAPTER 8

A Comparative Analysis of the Integrated Development Strategies in the Cases

The Bypass and the Experiential IDS

The cases described in the two previous chapters both provide examples of integrated development strategies or IDS. In the Alpha case the intervention was mainly of the bypass kind, while in the Beta case the consultants tended to proceed on experiential lines. Interventions cannot of course be categorized rigidly as belonging to the bypass or the experiential mode; most interventions will certainly encompass elements of both. But when we look back on any fairly lengthy change process it will be possible to see how much bypassing, relatively speaking, a consultant has undertaken.

Thus we would suggest that as a whole the Alpha case represented a bypass intervention, whereas the Beta case could be described as essentially experiential.

Assessment in Bypass and Experiential IDS as Exemplified in the Cases

Figure 8.1 illustrates the assessment phase in a bypass IDS (case Alpha), while Figure 8.2 shows the evolution of an experiential IDS (case Beta) during the same phase of learning.

In the Alpha case the assessment process began as part of the task process: the subject of the assignment was to help the client 'to design a market-planning system'. In the Beta case the discovery process started by tackling a behavioural problem: 'Help us to establish more constructive behaviour patterns between the holding company and its subsidiaries.' In both cases the beginnings on one side led to further analysis of the other: a task assessment led to an analysis of behaviour and a behavioural assessment led to the examination of tasks. So in both cases the impulse to further assessment came from an integration of task and behavioural elements.

The important difference is thus not that the interventionist starts by tackling a behavioural problem and then turns his attention to tasks, or vice versa. The main difference lies in the way the consultant chooses to integrate the two processes. By not sharing the integration process with the client, the interventionist gains time,

Assessment

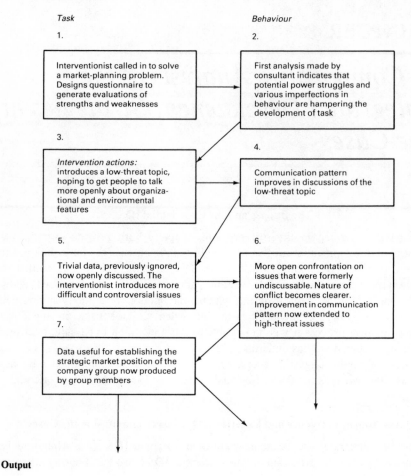

Task

1.

Interventionist called in to solve a market-planning problem. Designs questionnaire to generate evaluations of strengths and weaknesses

3.

Intervention actions: introduces a low-threat topic, hoping to get people to talk more openly about organizational and environmental features

5.

Trivial data, previously ignored, now openly discussed. The interventionist introduces more difficult and controversial issues

7.

Data useful for establishing the strategic market position of the company group now produced by group members

Behaviour

2.

First analysis made by consultant indicates that potential power struggles and various imperfections in behaviour are hampering the development of task

4.

Communication pattern improves in discussions of the low-threat topic

6.

More open confrontation on issues that were formerly undiscussable. Nature of conflict becomes clearer. Improvement in communication pattern now extended to high-threat issues

Output

Task

- Strategic assessment
- Evaluation of strengths and weaknesses
- Charting restrictions on growth

Behaviour

Interventionist discovers locked positions and manipulates the group to adopt a less rigid communication style and to venture on previously undiscussable topics.

Comments

- It became possible to assess many organizational weaknesses as various undiscussable topics were rendered discussable.
- The interventionist learned something of the mechanisms militating against open communications; he used his knowledge in planning ways of overcoming the obstacles to communication.
- Learning effects in the group were restricted to 'task-learning' about the strategic situation of the organization.

Figure 8.1. A model of the assessment phase in case Alpha (bypass integration)

Assessment

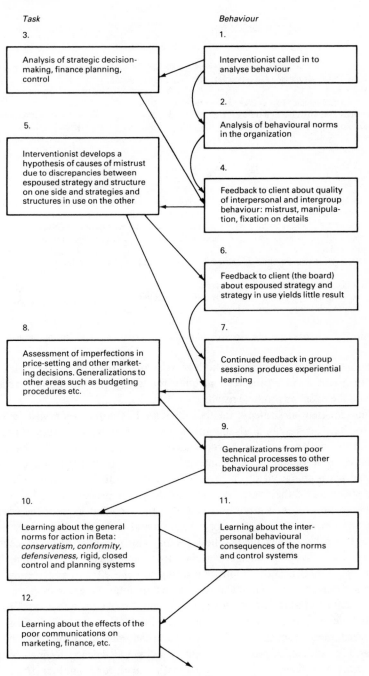

Figure 8.2. Continued on next page.

Output

Task

- Discovery of discrepancies between strategy and structure as espoused and implemented
- Strategic assessment: low degree of internal resources and unstable and difficult external conditions

Behaviour

- Mistrust, manipulation and fixation of details
- Learning how to learn about the organization
- Learning about the interdependence between behavioural norms, control systems and the handling of technical problems

Comments

- By acquiring a clearer insight into the discrepancies between the espoused strategy and policies and power structure on the one hand and those actually prevailing on the other, executives became aware of many of the reasons for the conflicts and poor communications.
- As they came to understand more about Beta's stressed situation, executives gave priority to prompt action.
- The interventionists continually shared their own insights with others, by:

  1. stating openly what they had observed;
  2. declaring openly what they mean by interdependence;
  3. inviting joint inquiries into behavioural and task processes.

Figure 8.2. A model of the assessment phase in case Beta (experiential integration)

and the intervention process will be less risky and upsetting in the initial phase. The consultant assumes the responsibility for taking the appropriate actions to constrain the client to produce results.

In an experiential strategy, on the other hand, the interventionist invites the client to share actively in analysing the nature of the task, the nature of prevailing behavioural modes, and the interdependence of the two. In the Alpha case the consultant soon found out that whatever he did as a pure marketing 'consultant', he would get nothing out of the group. So he started to inquire privately into the power structure of the company and into its group processes; he hypothesized that the group processes were influenced by the fact that each of the presidents had strong power positions in the organization and at the same time there was low interdependence between them. These factors and a conflict between centralists and decentralists had rendered certain topics undiscussable. He then decided among other things, and without consulting anyone else, to select some unforbidden low-threat topic to make at least a start on improving communications. As communications did in fact improve and certain discoveries about tasks began to be made, he ventured to introduce more serious high-threat topics and to try to make even these discussable. His idea was that once the group members had successfully analysed a problem together they would develop feelings of mutual trust; moreover their skill in communicating with one another should have increased sufficiently to allow for confrontation with increasingly controversial and difficult problems. And whether or not the consultant's hypothesis about the cause of the bad communications was valid, his plan worked. At any rate communications did improve. And not only that; the new skill in communications persisted and group members were gradually able to tackle more difficult problems. In this way they began to make important discoveries about their organization and about its strategic market position.

In the Beta case the consultant was engaged to cope with a problem of communications and discovered that the behavioural difficulties probably stemmed to a great extent from a discrepancy between the strategy and structure that were espoused and those that were actually in use. The consultant then confronted various people and groups in the organization with his discoveries, and he stated openly what he believed about the interdependence of task and behaviour. These first discoveries regarding behaviour and tasks led to new questions and subsequently to new discoveries. Thus in the Beta case the quality and scope of the learning increased as consultant and client alternated together between behaviour and tasks in a continual dialogue. But the process was more time-consuming than a bypass intervention would have been, and more upsetting for all the participants.

Invention and Realizations in a Bypass and an Experiential IDS

As we have seen, there are big differences in the two sorts of intervention strategy in the assessment phase, as illustrated in the cases of Alpha and Beta. Let us now look a little more closely at the invention and realization phases in the two cases (Figures 8.3 and 8.4).

Unlike the phase of assessment the phases of invention and realization as illustrated by our two cases reveal no apparent structural differences in the consultant's integration activities. In both cases the client started to invent new business strategies and to set new priorities on the product and market sides, and subsequently to implement the changes decided upon. In both cases the client evolved new behavioural norms, and the quality of interpersonal behaviour in the client organization continued to improve. Nevertheless these resemblances are superficial. We have seen that in the Alpha case certain shifts in strategy were suggested and eventually implemented. But these shifts fell well within the business concept that had already been prevailing in the organization for some time. There was no major alteration in the power structure, no change in important managerial posts, and no other changes likely to have a serious effect on any of those involved. Communications within the group and between group members and other companies had improved, but this was mainly because the organization had acquired a common language which made it easier to discuss product–market mix and competitive behaviour. It had also become permissible to discuss weaknesses and errors, at least within a narrow marketing-strategy context.

In the Beta case, however, the various discoveries were upsetting for all those concerned. First, the discovery of discrepancies between espoused strategies and

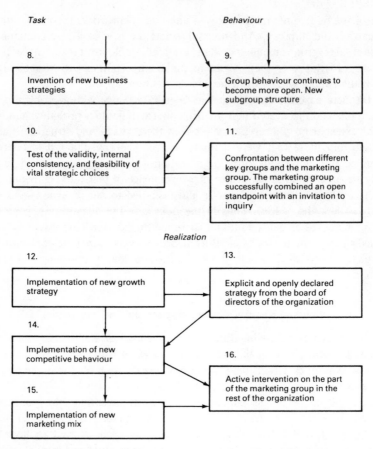

Figure 8.3. A model of the invention and realization phases in case Alpha

those actually in use made it necessary to choose one of them, which was not easy. The managing director chose to run the company according to his own convictions, with the result that four subsidiary managing directors left the organization; in three cases this meant abandoning their life's work. The changes in key norms, in power structure, in market orientation and so on were both substantial and profound. The various significant discoveries led to inventions and implementations of a far more comprehensive and all-embracing kind than Alpha had to face; in fact, far-reaching changes on this scale would probably have been impossible in an IDS tending towards the bypass model.

The question then arises as to whether such fundamental changes were really necessary in Beta. The first thing that can be said is that the changes were not just a whim of the managing director; they stemmed from well supported and reliable

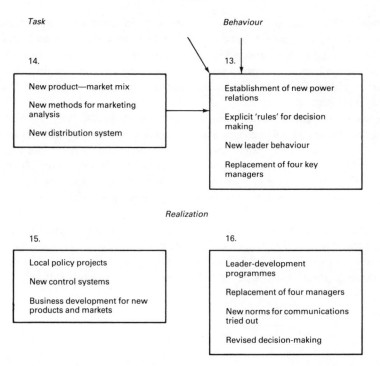

Figure 8.4. A model of the invention and realization phases in case Beta

findings about the changes that would be necessary in that sector of Swedish industry if it were to survive. The changes suggested by the managing director represented a threat to several of the company heads, who regarded traditional methods of production and sales as the only way of doing business in their industry. Thus when the conventional wisdom of this organization was called in question and it was decided that the strategy which top management had actually been applying was now also the espoused strategy, fundamental rethinking was involved for many of those concerned. No doubt they would all have had a much more comfortable life if these basic issues had never been questioned. But they would probably not have survived the tough competitive situation, or they might have done so but only by becoming dependent on government aid.

The assessment of the organizational and environmental uncertainty structures was another reason for the differences in the coping styles chosen by Alpha and Beta. Beta's stressed situation was reflected in the almost complete absence of intercompany solidarity, in the conflict between the owners and in the company's turbulent market situation. Prompt action was thus essential, and this triggered off several big changes in key management personnel.

In the case of Alpha, however, the group as a whole was enjoying fairly stable and predictable external conditions. Competitor reactions were predictable, the owner group was homogeneous, and developments on the market and structural developments in the value group were easy to foresee. It was the inadequate internal control systems, the internal power struggles and the uneven distribution of resources within Alpha that made this company a typical example of the 'disturbed' organization.

Thus different coping styles were necessary in Alpha and Beta. In Alpha the main problem was to pull the organization together and get its members to strive for the same goals. There was therefore less call for the interventionist to take risks. In the case of Beta, however, there was considerable uncertainty about what the owners really stood for and what they wanted, and at the same time conditions on the market were turbulent. Moreover the quality of the material and even some of the human resources, and of the organizational systems, was generally low.

In conclusion, it seems that the different types of problem in Alpha and Beta, the different status of the companies in terms of organizational and environmental uncertainty structures, and the different slant chosen in the integration development strategy probably all helped to determine the way the cases evolved.

CHAPTER 9

Epilogue – IDS in Future Action and Research

Effects of IDS

IDS, as we recall from its name, is a strategy for development. It therefore includes a certain number of rules that apply to development work and decision-making. But IDS can be pursued with varying degrees of skill, awareness, ambition, etc., and the actual outcome of any integrated development strategy will depend in great part on such factors and should be evaluated in terms of the particular project.

Compared with more traditionally conceived development projects, however, any strategy of integrated development should always, regardless of the specific context, achieve more in the following respects.

- IDS should generate a greater *understanding* of the task, more insight into behaviour, and greater awareness of the interdependence of task and behaviour.
- As a result of IDS people should *learn* more about organization–environment relations and about the connections between these and the relevant organizational culture.
- IDS encourages more open communication, which should help those involved to reach a *consensus* about what is wrong and about how the problems should be handled.
- As a result of the organizational learning that evolves in the course of working on an IDS, people should develop a heightened *readiness for action*; they will become more open to the idea of joint decision-making and more alert to the demands of effective action.

In addition to these effects, an IDS should leave all those who have been involved in it more aware of the importance of *learning* and more prone to continue to learn in future.

Challenges of IDS

Competence

Classic OD programmes have their own established techniques, methods, and test instruments. For policy formulation and the development of administrative

119

systems, tested methods and procedures are likewise available. Any of these methods may be useful in an IDS, but sometimes a method normally used in one discipline can have a detrimental effect when it is applied in another. A normal business policy questionnaire, for example, may have an inhibiting effect on creative group dynamics.

The challenge to anyone launching an IDS project in an organization is thus twofold: first, our IDS exponent should ideally command the theory and methods of the relevant behavioural disciplines and of the particular policy areas concerned, and, second, he should have sufficient knowledge of both these fields to be able to see when one theory or method counteracts another and to recognize any inherent inconsistencies or possible synergistic effects between two models. This kind of deeper insight can ultimately engender new theories and models.

The challenge of IDS lies in departing for the unknown. 'New' insights may mean insights that were not recognized as such at the outset. 'New' understanding may mean reaching some understanding of how to understand. 'New' methods may mean the discovery of new ways of creating new methods. Thus, to use Argyris' terminology, all IDS implies double loop learning. This represents a fundamental challenge to anyone who wants to develop himself as a professional practitioner or as a human being.

The demanding requirements should not, however, prevent anyone from adopting an IDS approach to development work. IDS should be regarded as an ideal to bear in mind and to strive for in most development work, rather than a uniform method to be applied only by some learned IDS expert. Anyone, regardless of his knowledge or the level of his awareness, can increase his capacity to work in the more 'integrated' way we have been discussing here. Every IDS exponent should start from his own level of competence. The first step for a technical expert might be to make a more explicit and systematic analysis of interpersonal behaviour during a group problem-solving process, and to try by employing some kind of bypass IDS to overcome the obstacles caused by bad group dynamics (see Chapter 6). For an OD expert, on the other hand, the challenge might consist of observing the task processes more carefully and trying with the help of an experiential IDS to identify the interdependence of the task and the behavioural processes (see Chapter 7). Thus, regardless of whether you start from the task or the behavioural end, the important thing is to alert yourself to the other viewpoint and to begin to make connections between the two.

Attitudes

There is a general tendency in the business world to concentrate on technical developments in hard times and to look to the human side when times are good. These reactions are misguided and result in the waste of both human and capital resources. It is certainly more difficult to advocate organizational learning and behavioural development at a time when turnover and profit figures are going down. That is when people tend to panic, perhaps calling for 'strong' leadership or blindly cutting costs, focusing narrowly on operations and engaging in a variety of financial manipulations. Management practices go 'hard'; only technical solutions are accepted, and even these have to be conventional and riskproof. At such a time all talk of learning is likely to be thought too soft, when in fact the search for the unconventional, a commitment to joint action, and a thoroughgoing process of organizational learning are just exactly what are needed.

To call for a technical drive in a period of prosperity is equally unpopular. The paramount organizational objectives at such times are to enhance the quality of working life and to enrich human relationships, all at the expense of strategic and technical development. Just when plentiful means are available for technical development, interest veers towards human relations: how to make people feel good at work, how to improve the management–worker relationship, how to pursuade corporations to respond to various social needs, and so on.

Thus the would-be exponents of IDS projects or of a more IDS-orientated way of thinking are likely to meet resistance for a number of reasons. The two attitudes described above, the hard and the soft, may be equally difficult to overcome. And there are other attitudes as well that may hamper or delay an IDS project, although these may not necessarily be overt. Some people may be unwilling to talk openly about what they are doing, for fear of disclosing technical incompetence; others may see the IDS as a threat to a power position that is perhaps based on secret agreements, the formation of factions, etc.

Whatever the attitudes might be that could hamper – or are already hampering – work on an integration development strategy, the best weapon with which to overcome them will be the essential and evident effectiveness of the IDS in question. It is difficult to find arguments against becoming more effective; moreover the aspiration to achieve the greatest possible efficiency by joint effort and for joint benefit is often strong enough to overcome many of the forces of resistance.

Decision-making

Structural changes in the organizational environment are putting increasing pressure on organizations to adapt. For an organization to adjust to change, the people who constitute the organization have to learn as a group to recognize the changes in their surroundings, to understand the significance and possible consequences of these, and to act on their knowledge.

The time when one man could scan the total environment and decide in splendid isolation what action to take, is long past. The world is too complex for any single person to grasp all factors affecting a large diversified company, and in any case people in organizations as well as outside them are no longer prepared to accept blindly the orders imposed on them from above. It is therefore vital that the people who constitute our organizations today should enter together upon a process of learning, so that consistent and effective joint action can be taken. The organizations that build up the best integrated learning systems are most likely to be the ones to survive and prosper.

Integrated development strategies of various kinds are already appearing, and are likely to become more common, in successful organizations all over the world. IDS is the key to adaptiveness, learning, and strategic change, and consequently to corporate survival and success. The explicit application of integrated development strategies as exemplified in this book will probably provide the most effective way for many corporations to do what will have to be done if their organizations are to survive.

We have illustrated cases here in which strategy formulation has been integrated with organizational development, administrative systems with social psychology, marketing with group dynamics, etc. These are examples from our own practice, derived from our own technical competence. We are convinced that many other applications are urgently called for and likely to be as fruitful as those described here. The political processes in government decision-making often deteriorate to the level of win–lose battles, withdrawals, and veto ploys. Crises at all levels – between the superpowers or between the members of a local council – are caused by a complex situation involving differing values, poor group dynamics, and almost total absence of mutual or joint learning, and the use of sloppy technical procedures that are never openly questioned. No one-sided structural change within the system will automatically make the processes of political decision-making more effective. Some form of IDS will have to be included, if the democratic political system is to find efficient modes of operation and, thus, to survive.

On account of the increasing complexity of the structural conditions of the modern world it is thus essential to improve the efficiency of decision-making, both the kind of organizational decision-making discussed in this book *and* the political decision-making of our local, national, and international bodies.

Effective decision-making needs to draw on the best technical competence available in a variety of specialist fields; it calls for collaboration and the exploitation of synergistic effects. Integrated strategies can provide the kind of multifaceted view necessary to success in complex decision-making.

Agents of IDS

Managers

Recent organizational research has confirmed what many people know from their own experience, namely that to be fully effective a manager must be strongly orientated both towards people and towards the task at hand. In this book we have shown how task processes and behavioural processes are in themselves interdependent, and how the effectiveness of the one will affect the functioning of the other. Thus, to be fully effective, a manager certainly needs to be simultaneously people-orientated and task-orientated, but he must also be capable – and this is even more important – of creating positive reinforcement between task-learning cycles and behavioural learning cycles.

This continual reinforcement back and forth between task learning and behavioural learning constitutes the very core of IDS. A manager committed to such a way of working will, among other things:

- learn to regard strategic planning, product development, marketing, and other spheres of action as organizational learning processes;
- create situations in which people can learn task and behavioural processes as a joint undertaking;
- be aware of the way in which organizational norms and control systems affect the organization's readiness to learn and adapt to a changing environment.

To succeed in these directions most managers will have to encourage in themselves a capacity to reflect upon their own roles in the organization and in their own task areas. Behavioural science theories and methods, business policy and other technical techniques will all be useful to this end. But even more important is a willingness to learn from what has actually happened; to examine events and reactions together with colleagues and others involved; to ponder upon different interpretations of events and listen to other people's interpretations.

To begin with this may well be too difficult in some of the more controversial domains. Working as consultants we have often found it advisable and feasible to start with some important but low-threat topic, until people begin to accept an IDS way of working. It then gradually becomes possible to tackle the more controversial and difficult questions more constructively.

Consultants

The intervention strategies employed by consultants are often classified in simplistic dichotomous terms such as 'expert or process', 'technical or behavioural', or 'client-orientated or purpose-orientated'. In this book we have advocated an integrated development strategy which imposes certain quite specific demands on the consultant. In order to develop his capacity to work along the lines required by an IDS, a consultant must be aware of his own need to learn and develop. In particular he should bear in mind the following.

- If his own opportunities for learning are to be exploited to the full in the course of his collaboration with the client, his consulting contract should be formulated so as to promote mutual learning and development.
- He must be prepared to learn by joining with other consultants, and with researchers and managers, in an open dialogue about counselling strategies and an honest scrutiny of actual consultant behaviour.

The principal idea here is that consultants must actually create situations in which they can learn about their own consulting theories and about any obstacles that are preventing them from taking effective action. Many consultants assume that their colleagues (for instance in a consulting agency) would be too competitive to engage in projects of this kind, and that the distance between consultants, managers, and researchers is too great for any such collaboration to prove fruitful. But to those consultants who have tried to design such learning situations, it has often come as a suprise to find that colleagues have been most helpful and that researchers and practitioners understand much more than is usually believed of them.

In the mutual model of consultation described in Chapter 4, the opportunities for the consultant to learn are particularly good. And learning is even more important to a consultant working along IDS lines than it is to another one using a more traditional approach, since the problem is not simply to learn a specific set of technical or behavioural methods; it is rather to learn how to learn, and to learn how to teach clients how to learn.

Researchers

Social scientists and researchers concerned with organizational effectiveness have traditionally separated thought from action, choosing comparative or case-study approaches to change. They either study organizations under different conditions, or they study 'change' as it is happening in a particular organization.

What distinguishes IDS from this approach is that the researcher becomes an interventionist, actively helping to plan and execute changes and thus simultaneously 'testing' aspects of his own theory. In our view this strategy can lead to change of an altogether more substantial kind. If the researcher is explicit about what he is doing and if his underlying principles are consistent and systematized, he will be able to feed back what he learns both to the client and to his colleagues. Looking briefly at the research element in IDS, we suggest that certain steps in this kind of development work and in other similar intervention strategies can, if systematically reported, make an important contribution to the fund of knowledge available to practitioners and researchers.

- The researcher must make an accurate diagnosis of the studied system in such a way as to explain why the system is as its is.
- The necessary changes, and the means by which they can be engendered, should be made explicit; it is therefore necessary to command – and to be able to expound – appropriate theories of change and intervention.
- In order to measure the effectiveness of the change or changes, theories of evaluation are required. These too must of course be made explicit.

These steps are naturally just as important in conventional organizational research as they are in integrated development strategies. But when the researcher is also an interventionist he is likely to use a more fragmented approach, aiming continuously to achieve a productive synthesis appropriate to practicable intervention activities. The choices made by the researcher/interventionist must therefore be openly discussed and explicated in considerable detail.

At all stages of an intervention process there are still many unsolved problems connected with techniques and skills. We need to find out more, for instance, about ways of creating effective learning environments while data-collection methods could also be greatly improved. As more material is reported by interventionists on these and other matters, it will become possible to make a systematic and realistic evaluation of the diverse research strategies in use.

Some Comments in Conclusion

What we in this book have dubbed IDS exists both as a practice and as a way of thinking. In explaining the reasons for the growing productivity of Japanese industry, Dr Takamia of the Japanese Productivity Centre gave pride of place to the successful integration of 'Gemeinschaft' with American managerial methods (reported from discussions at the Top Management Productivity Conference in Stockholm, May 1981). Dr Takamia explained that the preservation and continual development of the interpersonal group-behavioural patterns or traditional Japanese society was one of two components of success; the other was the particular approach to the technical problems of corporate planning, marketing, production technology, product development, and so on. But if productivity was to increase, these two components had to be successfully integrated. Where Japanese industry had enjoyed its greatest successes, this integration had also been particularly strong.

The Airbus project provides another example of successfully integrated development work. Very exacting technical requirements have been successfully satisfied in a project requiring close collaboration of experts from several European cultures and calling for the solution of some highly complex technical and managerial problems. In explaining the main reasons for this success, M. Beteille of the Airbus project stressed the following factors (in an interview with one of the present authors in 1980):

'People working on this project are highly motivated. It is true that we have different cultural backgrounds, but we all speak a common language – the technical language. We must also all of us accept the "final" test – which is the same for a Frenchman, a German or an Englishman – will the aircraft fly? The ultimate goal which we all share has helped us overcome several of the cultural and managerial problems – not that we have solved them all – but we have learned how to live with them and in the meantime still make aircraft that can fly.'

The Airbus project and Japanese industry are far removed from one another geographically and in many other ways; none the less they share an important ingredient: in both cases, technically advanced production techniques are being applied in social settings characterized by highly complex cultural patterns. And as we discussed in Chapter 2 above, several major contemporary development trends are adding everywhere to the complexity of technical problem-solving and of social relationships. In both the cases quoted, the Airbus project and Japanese industry, it is the techniques for integrating advanced technical development with the relevant social systems that have been the key to success.

In this book we have explored in some detail various ways in which managers, consultants, and researchers in modern corporations can increase the effectiveness of their development activities. We hope that the integrated development strategy will provide all these three categories with insights and methods appropriate to handling the increasing complexities of organizational development.

References

Andrews, K. R. (1971). *The Concept of Corporate Strategy*, Irwin, Homewood IU.

Ansoff, I. H. (1975). *Corporate Strategy*, McGraw-Hill, New York.

Ansoff, I. H. (1978). *Strategic Management*, Macmillan, London.

Argyris, C. (1964). *Integrating the Individual and the Organization*, Wiley, New York.

Argyris, C. (1970). *Intervention Theory and Method*, Addison-Wesley, Reading, Mass.

Argyris, C. (1976). *Increasing Leadership Effectiveness*, Wiley, New York.

Argyris, C. and Schön, D. (1974). *Theory in Practice*, Jossey-Bass, San Francisco.

Argyris, C. and Schön, D. (1978). *Organizational Learning*, Addison-Wesley, Reading, Mass.

Asplund, Gisèle (1974). *Osäkerhetsfaktorer i företaget och i dess miljö*, EFI, Stockholm.

Asplund, Göran (1975). *Strategy Formulation*, EFI, Stockholm.

Bales, R. F. and Strodtbeck, F. L. (1968). Phases in Group Problem Solving. In Cartwright, D. and Zander, A. (eds) *Group Dynamics*, Harper and Row, New York.

Beckhard, R. (1969). *Organization Development*, Addison-Wesley, Reading Mass.

Beckhard, R. and Harris, R. (1977). *Organizational Transitions*, Addison-Wesley, Reading, Mass.

Blake, R. and Mouton, J. (1974). *The Managerial Grid*, Gulf Publishing Co, Houston, Texas.

Chandler, A. (1962). *Strategy and Structure*, MIT Press, Cambridge, Mass.

Hersey, P. and Blanchard, K. H. (1972). *Management of Organizational Behavior*, Prentice-Hall, Englewood Cliffs NJ.

Hofer, C. and Schendel, D. (1978). *Strategy Formulation – Analytical Concepts*, West Publishing Co, St Paul, Minnesota.

Katz, R. L. (1970). *Cases and Concepts in Corporate Strategy*, Prentice-Hall, Englewood Cliffs, N.J.

Reddin, W. (1970). *Managerial Effectiveness*, McGraw-Hill, New York.

Schein, E. (1969). *Process Consultation*, Addison-Wesley, Reading Mass.

Vroom, V. (1964). *Work and Motivation*, Wiley, New York.

Vroom, V. and Yetton, P. (1973). *Leadership and Decision Making*, University of Pittsburgh Press.

Index